NAOSHIMA TRAVEL GUIDE
2024

Naoshima Unveiled: Your Comprehensive
Travel Companion to Island of Tranquility:
Discover the Hidden Gems, Adventures,
Cultural Oasis, and Artistic Tapestry

Mark E. Fears

Table Of Contents

My Naoshima Vacation

Traveling to Naoshima turned out to be a life-changing and wonderful holiday that combined art, nature, and cultural immersion seamlessly. I was enthralled by this island in Japan's Seto Inland Sea from the moment I got off the ship because of its distinct vibe and the possibility of an amazing trip.

The first thing that caught my attention was how well modern art was incorporated into the island's natural scenery. The visionary architect Tadao Ando's Benesse House Museum, a combination museum and hotel, served as the inspiration for my artistic investigation. As I strolled around its galleries, I came across works of art by well-known artists, many of which were thoughtfully positioned to enhance the surrounding natural beauty. The Chichu Art Museum offered a private and immersive experience with works by Monet and other great artists. It is tucked away underground and features minimalistic architecture.

The Art House Project, where traditional residences were converted into engaging art pieces, was one of the highlights of my trip to Naoshima. It was like entering a dream world to stroll around these rooms because each house used art to tell a different story. Seeing how modern ingenuity and the island's antique architecture interacted was an exciting experience.

The dedication of Naoshima to sustainability gave my visit a deeper meaning. All of the eco-friendly activities, including recycling and using renewable energy, fit in with the island's general philosophy of harmony between people and the environment. My relationship with the environment was improved by this focused attitude, which made each exploration meaningful and enriching.

Beyond the artwork, Naoshima's immaculate beaches and picturesque walking paths provided peaceful moments. Because of the small nature of the island, I was able to discover its hidden treasures, which ranged from serene temples to surprising artworks buried away in quiet places. My favorite way to get around was to rent a bicycle, which allowed me to travel at a leisurely pace and take in the breathtaking scenery and unexpected works of art that were waiting around every corner.

I immersed myself in the community by going to festivals and activities that honored community and creativity. These events offered a rare glimpse into the heart of Naoshima, a city where art had become a vital aspect of daily life rather than being restricted to museums.

Naoshima was more than just a vacation spot for me when I departed on the ferry back to the mainland; it was a profound voyage of self-discovery, artistic enlightenment, and a peaceful connection with a location that masterfully blends tradition and innovation. Naoshima was now more than just a place on a map; it was a haven of inspiration that I would carry with me long after the ferry departed.

1. Introduction

1.1 About Naoshima

A small island in Japan's Seto Inland Sea, Naoshima offers a singular fusion of modern art, tranquil scenery, and cultural diversity. Known as the "Art Island," Naoshima is a refuge for both nature lovers and art fans due to its avant-garde artworks, which have won international praise.

The island's metamorphosis started in the 1990s when the Benesse Corporation and well-known architect Tadao Ando started a bold proposal to convert Naoshima into an outdoor art gallery. Presently, tourists may see a tasteful fusion of contemporary art and conventional Japanese architecture, as museums like the Benesse House Museum and the Chichu Art Museum mix in perfectly with the island's scenic surroundings.

Naoshima is more than just a place to see art; it's a canvas where modern artistry combines with the enduring beauty of nature. The island's landscape is given a strange twist by The Art House Project, a collection of abandoned houses transformed into art pieces. Wandering around these remodeled areas, visitors may see how art and daily life coexist.

Beyond its artistic charm, Naoshima provides a peaceful haven from the bustle of the city. The island's gorgeous beaches, verdant surroundings, and breathtaking sunsets foster a tranquil setting that invites guests to deeply engage with both art and nature.

1.2 Synopsis of History

Naoshima's traditional fishing towns and maritime heritage play a significant role in the city's history. The island changed throughout time from a sleepy fishing community to a well-known hub for modern art on a global scale.

The concept that would smoothly blend art, architecture, and nature was envisioned in the 1980s by the Japanese publishing and education organization Benesse Corporation, which marked a turning point in the field. The company, led by Soichiro Fukutake, worked with architect Tadao Ando to develop a distinctive cultural area on Naoshima.

The 1992 establishment of the Benesse House, a hotel and museum, marked the beginning of the island's transformation as a destination for art. This was the beginning of Naoshima's transformation into an unmatched cultural center.

The Art House Project, Lee Ufan Museum, and Chichu Art Museum were later added, further enhancing Naoshima's reputation as a refuge for fans of modern art. The island has become a model of effective cultural revival due to its dedication to upholding its traditional legacy while welcoming modernity. As a testament to the ability of art to change a place's identity and fate, Naoshima stands today.

1.3 Why Go to Naoshima?

Tucked away in Japan's Seto Inland Sea, the enchanting island of Naoshima skillfully combines modern art, tranquil scenery, and traditional charm. Known worldwide as the "Art Island," this creative sanctuary attracts tourists from all over the world who want to fully immerse themselves in the local culture.

Naoshima's main attraction is its outstanding art museums and outdoor installations that blend in perfectly with the island's scenic surroundings. Constructed by the acclaimed architect Tadao Ando, the Benesse House Museum is a masterpiece in and of itself, containing a remarkable collection of modern art. Another architectural treasure is the Chichu Art Museum, which adopts a subterranean strategy to blend in with the surroundings while displaying pieces by artists such as James Turrell and Claude Monet.

Outside the museums, Naoshima's open-air areas function as independent galleries. By transforming traditional Japanese residences into site-specific installations, The Art House Project integrates art into the architecture of the island. Sculptures adorn charming communities, offering visitors an immersive experience where art is artfully incorporated into everyday life.

The festivals on the island, including the Setouchi Triennale, a significant contemporary art event held every three years, demonstrate the island's dedication to the arts. Naoshima transformed into a vibrant center of innovation during this period, presenting a wide range of installations and events that add to the city's rich cultural fabric.

Not only is Naoshima a haven for art enthusiasts, but it's also a peaceful getaway. A peaceful ambiance that encourages reflection and relaxation is created by the contrast of modern art installations, calm beaches, and traditional Japanese architecture.

For those who appreciate art or are just looking for a distinctive cultural getaway, Naoshima provides an unmatched fusion of creativity, environment, and customs. Because of the island's dedication to the symbiosis of art and environment, it is a place that defies conventional tourist stereotypes and invites travelers to discover the meeting point of modern expression and classic beauty.

1.4 Information to Know Before Leaving

It is advisable to familiarize yourself with the following details before traveling to Naoshima to make the most of your stay on this special island:

1. **Art Island Concept**: Because of its substantial collection of modern artwork, Naoshima is frequently called the "Art Island". As you travel the island, be prepared to come across a lot of museums and art installations.

2. **Benesse House Accommodation**: Take into consideration booking a room at the Benesse House, a

distinctive lodging option that blends a hotel and a museum. This architectural wonder gives visitors unique access to the museums before and after regular business hours and provides an immersive art experience.

3. **Reservations for the Chichu Art Museum**: To preserve a calm environment, the Chichu Art Museum restricts the amount of visitors. To ensure your admission, it's best to book reservations in advance.

4. **Art House Project**: Discover how traditional Japanese homes are being converted into modern art spaces at the Art House Project. Naoshima boasts a unique artistic landscape enhanced by the unique installations seen in each residence.

5. **Setouchi Triennale**: Every three years, a significant art festival, check out the itinerary for the Setouchi Triennale. Schedule your visit at this time to see a wider selection of performances and art installations.

6. **Ferry Schedule**: Uno Port in Okayama Prefecture is the ferry port from which Naoshima is reachable. As the frequency of the ferries varies based on the season and time of day, make sure to check the timetable in advance, especially if you have specific plans.

7. **Rental Bicycles**: If you want to see the island at your speed, think about hiring a bicycle. Because of its small size and well-kept roads, cycling is a great method to get around Naoshima and visit art installations and museums.

8. Enjoy the cuisine of the island at the cafes and restaurants serving **Local Cuisine**. Particularly, seafood dishes highlight the finest harvests from the Seto Inland Sea.

9. **Weather Considerations**: Pay attention to the weather, particularly if you intend to see outdoor art exhibits. It's crucial to wear comfortable clothing, wear sunscreen, and stay hydrated, especially in the warmer months.

10. **Behave with Respect**: When visiting the cultural venues and art installations, act with respect. Respect the quiet environment that Naoshima is known for and follow any rules that museums may set.

Traveling to Naoshima is a unique experience because of its unique fusion of art, nature, and traditional charm. Through previous planning and a commitment to the island's creative culture, you may fully experience the diversity of cultures that make this alluring place so fascinating.

2. Essential Planning For Naoshima

2.1 The Ideal Time to Go to Naoshima

The ideal time to explore Naoshima is during the spring and fall seasons when the weather is mild and the island's natural beauty is at its peak. When deciding when to visit Naoshima, you should take into account both weather conditions and cultural events to maximize your experience on the "Art Island."

- **Spring (March to May):** As cherry blossoms bloom in the spring, Naoshima is transformed into a charming setting. The pleasant weather, which ranges from 10 to 20 degrees Celsius (50 to 68 degrees Fahrenheit), makes exploring outside enjoyable. With cherry blossoms in the background, the Art House Project and outdoor works take on an even more magical quality.

-**Fall (September to November):** Another great time to visit Naoshima is in the fall. The range of temperatures is 15 to 25 degrees Celsius (59 to 77 degrees Fahrenheit), providing comfortable conditions for outdoor pursuits. The island's overall appearance is improved by the autumn leaves, which give it a splash of color. If it happens to be held in the fall, there's also the chance to see a wide range of installations of modern art at the Setouchi Triennale.

Although certain times of year are said to be ideal, Naoshima's museums and art installations are open all year round, and every season has its special beauty. Though hot and muggy at times, summer (June to August) is a great season for beach activities. For those looking for a more tranquil experience, winter (December to February) is quieter, while certain outdoor installations might not be as enticing in the colder months.

2.2 Visa And Entry requirements

Visitors who intend to visit Naoshima should be informed about Japan's entry restrictions and visa requirements. varying nationalities are subject to varying admission criteria in Japan.

- **Visa Requirement:** Many nationals, including those of the US, Canada, and the majority of European nations, are exempt from the need for a visa to enter Japan for brief visits, often lasting up to 90 days. The specific laws may, however, differ, therefore it's important to confirm the most recent criteria on the official website of the Japanese embassy or consulate in your nation of residence.

-**Passport Validity:** Verify that your passport will be valid for a minimum of six months after the day you intend to depart Japan.

-**Visa for Longer Stays:** You might need to get the necessary visa before your trip if you intend to stay in Japan for a longer period than is permitted without a visa, or if you are going there for job or study-related reasons. Longer stays may have more complicated requirements, such as supplementary paperwork.

- **COVID-19 Travel limitations:** In light of the current world circumstances, make sure you are compliant with any COVID-19-related travel limitations. Japan has taken action to stop the virus's spread, and admission requirements might alter.

2.3 Length of Visit

How long you should spend on Naoshima will depend on your interests, how quickly you want to explore, and which events or festivals you want to attend. Some prefer to immerse themselves more deeply in the island's distinct environment, while others spend a day touring the main art attractions.

- **Day excursion:** If you have limited time, you could consider taking a day excursion to Naoshima. This enables you to see important sites including the Art House Project, the Benesse House Museum, and the Chichu Art Museum. But remember that one day could feel too short and you might not have time to see everything the island has to offer.

- **Two to Three Days:** Allow two to three days to thoroughly experience Naoshima's art scene. This makes it possible to explore the island more slowly, taking the time to take in the peaceful atmosphere and visiting other museums and outdoor installations. If any festivals or cultural events take place while you're there, you can also take part in them.

- **Extended Stay:** An extended stay of four days or more offers the chance to delve further into Naoshima's art and culture for those looking for a more immersive experience or hoping to attend events such as the Setouchi Triennale. This makes it possible to explore nearby islands at a slower pace and to establish a stronger bond with the locals.

For however long you stay, Naoshima offers a unique combination of modern art, scenic beauty, and cultural activities. To fully experience this exceptional location, organize your stay taking into account your tastes and schedule.

2.4 Money and Exchange of Currencies

Knowing the local currency, accepted forms of payment, and available currency exchange locations on the island is crucial while making travel plans to Naoshima. The Japanese Yen (JPY) is the official currency of Japan. Although major credit cards are accepted everywhere and at larger establishments, since Naoshima is a small island, it is best to have cash on hand for smaller shops, local markets, and other locations that might not take cards.

- **Currency Exchange:** Major airports, banks, and currency exchange offices in places such as Tokyo or Okayama (the entry point to Naoshima) offer currency exchange services. Before visiting the island, it is advised to convert some of your cash into Japanese Yen so that you have cash on hand for convenience.

- **ATMs:** There aren't many ATMs in Naoshima, and not all of them take foreign credit cards. If possible, get funds out of bigger cities before visiting the island.

Furthermore, certain establishments and lodging providers could favor payments made in cash.

- **Credit Cards:** While many larger shops, restaurants, and hotels on Naoshima accept credit cards, smaller establishments sometimes prefer cash payments. Having a mix of cash and credit cards on hand is a smart idea for covering a range of costs.

- **Traveler's Checks:** It can be difficult to locate businesses that accept traveler's checks because they are not as widely utilized in Japan. It is best to use cards in addition to cash for your transactions.

If you want to use your credit or debit cards in Japan, let your bank know in advance to avoid any possible problems with transactions being viewed as suspicious. This guarantees a seamless financial encounter throughout your visit to Naoshima.

2.5 Language And Communication

Even though English is taught in schools, not everyone in Naoshima can speak it fluently. Japanese is the official language of Japan. But because the island is becoming more and more popular with tourists from abroad, English-speaking personnel may be found working in many tourism-oriented establishments, such as hotels and prominent tourist destinations.

Tips for Language:

1. **Fundamental Phrases:** You can have a better experience if you know a few fundamental Japanese phrases. In communication, simple expressions like "hello" (konnichiwa), "thank you" (arigatou gozaimasu), and "goodbye" (sayonara) can make a big difference.

2. **Translation Apps:** To overcome linguistic barriers, think about utilizing translation apps on your smartphone. These applications can help with spoken communication facilitation and written text translation.

3. **English Signage:** Though not everywhere, English-language signage and information are available, particularly in tourist-heavy regions.

4. **Politeness:** Courtesies are highly valued in Japanese society. Positive relationships can be facilitated by using courteous language and gestures, like a small bow.

5. **Patience and Understanding**: Try to be understanding and patient when dealing with linguistic barriers. Locals value effort, and communication difficulties can be resolved with a kind demeanor.

You may easily travel to Naoshima and engage in meaningful encounters with the local people by keeping an eye on the language context and utilizing these helpful ideas.

2.6 Essentials and Packing Advice

The island of Naoshima offers a unique combination of art, nature, and cultural activities, therefore packing appropriately is important. The following packing advice is crucial to a relaxing and pleasurable stay:

Apparel:

1. **Comfortable Walking Shoes:** Some are walking around Naoshima, particularly if you want to see the outdoor art pieces. Sturdy, comfortable shoes are a must.

2. **Weather-Appropriate Attire:** Verify the predicted weather for the days you will be traveling. For warmer months, bring clothing that is airy and light, and for colder months, think about layering.

3. **Swimwear:** If you intend to enjoy the beaches or any water-based activities when visiting during the warmer months, remember to pack swimwear.

Examination of Art:

1. **Camera and Binoculars:** Take in the splendor of the picturesque scenery and art installations. Having binoculars can improve your experience, particularly if you're looking at outdoor exhibitions.

2. **Daypack or Tote Bag:** Bring water, sunscreen, a guidebook, and other necessities in a compact daypack or tote bag for your island exploration.

3. **Reusable Water Bottle:** Drink plenty of water, particularly when visiting outdoor sites. Reusable water bottles can help reduce your influence on the environment.

Utilitarian Fundamentals:

1. **Adapters and Chargers:** Make sure the power adapters you own are compatible with the devices you use. In order to record and share your adventures, chargers for phones, cameras, and other devices are necessary.

2. **Travel Insurance:** It is advisable to have travel insurance that includes coverage for trip cancellations and medical emergencies. Verify the coverage details to make sure you are fully protected.

3. **Prescription Medications:** Pack a basic first aid kit and a sufficient supply of any prescription medications you may require while visiting.

A Cultural Perspective:
1. **Modest Attire:** It is appreciated to wear modest clothing when visiting cultural sites or mingling with locals. Always have a lightweight shawl or scarf on hand to cover your shoulders if needed.

2. **Respectful Accessory:** Be aware that some art spaces could have special guidelines, like no taking pictures. For sun protection, bring along accessories like a hat or sunglasses.

Additional Items:
1. **Travel handbook:** A travel handbook with details on Naoshima's culinary selections, art attractions, and customs can prove to be a useful tool.

2. **Travel record:** Keep a record of your thoughts and experiences while traveling. Naoshima's distinct climate could stimulate artistic expression.

If you take into account the unique features of Naoshima's attractions, weather, and cultural quirks, you may pack light and guarantee a well-planned and pleasurable trip to an island steeped in art.

3. Naoshima's Culinary Treats and Drinks

3.1 Regional Foods and Specialties

Naoshima's cuisine scene offers a beautiful fusion of fresh seafood, locally produced products, and creative flair, reflecting the island's balanced blend of tradition and contemporary. The fishing sector plays a major role in the island's rich culinary legacy, with an abundance of fresh seafood taking center stage in many meals.

A. **Delicious Seafood:**

1. * **Seasonal Seafood:** Because of its coastal location, Naoshima has access to an abundance of seasonal seafood, including melt-in-your-mouth whitebait, exquisite sea urchins, juicy oysters, and spiny lobsters.

2. * **Monjayaki:** Made with a batter of wheat flour, water, and dashi (Japanese fish broth), monjayaki is a savory pancake that is a local delicacy. A hot griddle is used to cook the batter, which is then covered with cheese, chopped veggies, and fish.

3. * **Sea Bream Tempura:** A crispy and savory meal that highlights the freshness of local seafood, sea bream tempura is lightly battered and deep-fried.

4. * **Shirauo:** A specialty of Naoshima, these translucent white bait fish are generally eaten raw or very lightly grilled. They are a well-liked appetizer or main meal because of their subtle flavor and crisp texture.

5. * **Akoebi:** The sweet and luscious meat of this red shrimp is highly valued. They are typically served grilled or sashimi.

B. **Traditional Recipes Using Local Ingredients:**

1. * **Olive Products:** Olive oil is a mainstay in local cuisine, and olives are one of Naoshima's most famous exports. Dressing salads, marinating meats, and enhancing the flavor of many foods are all done with olive oil.

2. * **Handmade Noodles:** With a long history of producing noodles, handmade noodles are a well-liked treat in Naoshima. To highlight the delicate flavors of the ingredients, these noodles are frequently served in straightforward broths or stir-fries.

3. * **Seasonal Vegetables:** The rich soil of Naoshima yields a wide range of seasonal vegetables, which are frequently used in regional cuisine. Naoshima's food is enhanced by the vivid flavors and colors of fresh vegetables, including sun-ripened tomatoes, crisp cucumbers, and soft greens.

4. * **Sake and Shochu:** Deeply rooted in Japanese culture, sake and shochu are distilled alcoholic beverages that are manufactured locally and are available in

Naoshima. These drinks are frequently served with traditional dishes, giving the meal a dash of refinement and regional flair.

C. Island Mainstays and Customary Cuisine

In addition to seafood, Naoshima's cuisine offers a range of island mainstays and traditional dishes that capture the essence of the region's way of life and cultural influences.

1. * **Momiji Manju:** A popular Naoshima delicacy, these steamed buns are shaped like maple leaves and filled with sweet red bean paste.

2. * **Sanuki Udon:** A mainstay of Naoshima cuisine, this substantial wheat noodle dish comes from the nearby prefecture of Kagawa. Typically, a hot soup with a variety of toppings is served with the chewy noodles.

3. * **Shiozake:** A traditional meal with a salty and umami flavor, prepared from fermented rice bran and sea

urchin. It is frequently used as a side dish with rice or veggies.

D. **Culinary Arts Exhibitions:**

The artistic character of the island is reflected in Naoshima's culinary scene, where a lot of eateries take pleasure in serving up their food in an original way. Chefs frequently use modern art elements in their plates, turning simple meals into works of visual art with vibrant garnishes, elaborate layouts, and distinctive serving utensils.

Apart from its delicious food, Naoshima has a lovely assortment of cafes and tea houses where guests may unwind and take in the peaceful atmosphere of the island. These places offer a lovely break from discovering the island's artwork and natural beauty, frequently serving locally sourced cuisine and traditional Japanese sweets.

Whether you're looking for a taste of fresh seafood, a traditional Japanese dinner, or a culinary experience inspired by art, Naoshima's eclectic culinary scene has something to tempt your taste buds. A wonderful trip into the heart of Naoshima's history and heritage is guaranteed with every dining experience because of the island's dedication to using fresh ingredients, regional flavors, and artistic expression.

3.2 Vegan and Vegetarian Selections

Not only is Naoshima known for its fresh seafood and traditional Japanese fare, but it also offers a wide range of delicious and fulfilling options for vegetarians and vegans. Plant-based meals that highlight the tastes and textures of the area are becoming more and more popular on the island because of their dedication to sustainability and love for local cuisine.

A. **Vegetable Treasures:**

1.* **Vegetarian Bento Boxes:** A traditional Japanese dinner filled with a variety of plant-based cuisine, vegetarian bento boxes are available at many eateries. Rice, pickled veggies, seaweed, tofu, and a range of other vegetarian alternatives are frequently included in these boxes, which make for a filling and tasty supper.

2. * **Vegetable Tempura:** A vegetarian take on the traditional tempura meal, vegetable tempura consists of a range of seasonal vegetables that are perfectly crispy and gently breaded before being deep-fried. The options are infinite, ranging from bell peppers and carrots to eggplant and zucchini.

3. * **Tofu Stews:** The star of hearty tofu stews is tofu, a mainstay of Japanese cooking. Simmered in a fragrant broth with a variety of veggies, these stews provide a hearty and filling dish.

4. * **Vegetable Sushi and Maki Rolls:** Making sushi and maki rolls from scratch is a tasty and inventive way to eat more plant-based food. These sushi variations,

made with cucumber, avocado, carrots, and other fresh veggies, are sure to satisfy even the pickiest eaters.

B. Vegetarian Selections:

1. * *Vegan Salads: With so many fresh vegetables available, Naoshima offers colorful and delectable vegan salads. When combined with different types of greens, veggies, and plant-based dressings, these salads provide a wholesome and filling dish.

2. * **Vegan Ramen:** Though typically made with meat, vegan ramen has become more and more well-liked in recent years. These substantial vegan noodles and savory plant-based broth make for a satisfying and flavorful lunch that is loaded with veggies and tofu.

3. * **Vegan Curry:** A popular dish in Japanese cooking, vegan curries offer a filling and delicious plant-based alternative. These dishes, which are cooked

with a variety of veggies, tofu, and a decadent vegan curry sauce, will cheer you up.

4. * **Vegan Sweets and Desserts:** Everyone can enjoy a sweet treat thanks to Naoshima's extensive vegan cuisine scene. You can find plenty of solutions to fulfill any sweet craving, from plant-based mochi to vegan ice cream.

Naoshima's food scene is changing to suit a range of dietary needs as the city draws tourists from all over the world. A great range of vegetarian and vegan alternatives that satisfy a variety of tastes and dietary concerns are available at Naoshima, a restaurant that prides itself on using fresh ingredients, local produce, and inventive culinary approaches. Every traveler may find something to enjoy in Naoshima's food scene, whether they're looking for a taste of inventive plant-based cuisine or a classic Japanese dinner.

3.3 Sake Tasting and Regional Drinks

Situated in the middle of the Seto Inland Sea, the island of Naoshima is well-known not only for its long sake-making legacy but also for its art and culture. The island is home to several sake breweries that create carefully produced sake using regional ingredients and special brewing methods.

A. **Naoshima Sake Culture:**

In Naoshima culture, sake, a traditional rice wine from Japan, has a particular significance. The island's sake breweries have been making premium sake using traditional techniques and ingredients that have been sourced locally for generations. The unique flavor and scent of Naoshima sake are a result of the island's environment and water quality, which are thought to be perfect for making sake.

B. **Events Related to Taste Testing:**

Sake tastings are available at many breweries on Naoshima, introducing guests to the world of this fine libation. A range of sakes are usually sampled during these tastings, and each is matched with regional specialties that enhance the flavors and fragrances of the sake.

C. **Nearby Breweries and Their Area of Expertise:**

1. * **Kikunomasu Brewery:** This well-known brewery crafts a range of sake varieties, among them Junmai Daiginjo, a premium sake prized for its subtle flavor and scent.

2. * **Honjo Brewery** is well-known for producing Nama-sake, an unpasteurized sake that keeps its flavors bright and lively.

3. * **Kido Brewery:** This brewery specializes in Koshu, a red rice-based sake with an earthy flavor and distinctive amber hue.

D. **Additional Local Drinks:**

In addition to sake, Naoshima has a variety of other regional drinks that are well worth trying.

1.* **Shochu:** A favorite choice among the natives, shochu is a distilled alcohol that is usually manufactured from rice, sweet potatoes, or barley.

2. * **Umeboshi Plum Wine:** This tart and sweet wine is made from umeboshi plums and has a distinct flavor of local food from Naoshima.

3. * **Green Tea:** Naoshima is renowned for producing excellent green tea, which is a tasty and pleasant beverage.

E. **Sake Pairing:**

Consider consuming Naoshima's sake with regional specialties that enhance its flavor profile to get the most out of it.

1. * **Seafood:** The subtle flavors of sake blend well with the freshness of Naoshima's seafood.

2. * **Tempura:** The umami flavors of sake are complemented by the crispy and delicious tempura, a famous Japanese meal.

3. * **Tofu:** The flavor of sake is enhanced by the mild and adaptable tofu.

A unique and original experience, Naoshima's sake-making tradition and wide range of locally produced beverages let guests enjoy the island's rich culinary legacy and understand the craft of sake brewing.

4. Naoshima's Restaurant and Nightlife Scene

4.1 The Greatest Fine Dining Restaurants

Beyond its traditional Japanese cuisine, Naoshima offers a wide range of fine dining options to suit even the most discriminating palate. These eateries highlight the island's dedication to using only the freshest, most inventive ingredients in their dishes, as well as their sophisticated dining settings.

***1. Benesse House's Terrace Restaurant: ** Located inside the well-known Benesse House Museum, the Terrace Restaurant presents a tasteful fusion of fine dining and art. With sweeping views of the Seto Inland Sea, the restaurant serves fine French cuisine that is made with seasonal ingredients.

***2. The Island Table:** Offering a secluded and elegant dining experience, The Island Table is situated in the serene environs of the Benesse Art Site Naoshima. Modern European cuisine is featured on the restaurant's menu, with a focus on locally sourced fish and seasonal products.

****3. **Il Posto di Naoshima: This Italian restaurant infuses Naoshima's culinary scene with a hint of Europe. The menu at Il Posto di Naoshima offers traditional Italian fare that is made using local, fresh ingredients to create a delicious blend of Italian and Japanese flavors.

***4. Gochi-So Bancha: **A traditional Japanese kaiseki dining experience can be had at this establishment, which is tucked away in the lovely Honmura neighborhood. Kaiseki is a multi-course meal that displays the chef's skill in the kitchen. Seasonal ingredients are used to create a visually spectacular and delectable culinary trip.

*5. La Cucina di Naoshima: ** This restaurant serves real Italian food and has a view of the charming port of Honmura. Fresh seafood, homemade pasta dishes, and wood-fired pizzas are all served at the restaurant using authentic Italian cooking methods.

6* Ebisu Kami: Authentic Japanese food is served at this traditional Japanese restaurant. The restaurant serves sushi, tempura, and sashimi among other foods, and also has a tatami room dining space.

**7* Aisunao: Aisunao is a Michelin-starred eatery that serves inventive Japanese food on a tasting menu. The restaurant creates visually stunning and delectable dishes by utilizing traditional cooking techniques along with locally sourced ingredients.

8* Okonomiyaki Umikko: Known for its delicious Japanese pancakes made with flour, eggs, and cabbage, Okonomiyaki Umikko is a well-liked dining establishment. The restaurant's okonomiyaki is well-known for its crispy texture and tasty sauce, and it offers a wide selection of toppings.

Savoring great meals while taking in the tranquil setting of Naoshima is possible at these upscale restaurants, which give a window into the island's sophisticated culinary scene.

4.2 Eateries and Neighborhood Restaurants

Naoshima boasts a thriving array of local eateries and casual eating alternatives that perfectly balance the island's unique flavors and laid-back attitude with its fine dining scene. Discover the essence of Naoshima's culinary culture in a cozy and inviting environment while savoring the freshness of regional products at these restaurants.

***1. Udon Honmura:** Tucked away in the Honmura neighborhood, this quaint eatery offers classic udon noodles with an assortment of toppings and broths. The restaurant is well-liked by both locals and tourists because of its cozy atmosphere and substantial udon dishes.

***2. The delicious Japanese pancake known as okonomiyaki, which is created with flour, eggs, and a variety of toppings, is the specialty of Okonomiyaki Ben, a local favorite in Naoshima. The restaurant is a must-try for casual dining because of its welcoming ambiance and delicious okonomiyaki meals.

****3. **Café Terrace:** Conveniently located close to the Honmura harbor, Cafe Terrace provides a quaint environment for indulging in a small lunch or a cool drink. A variety of coffee, tea, sandwiches, and salads are available on the cafe's menu, all of which are served with a view of the Seto Inland Sea.

***4. Restaurant Honmura: This cozy, family-owned eatery offers traditional Japanese fare in a cozy setting. The restaurant's menu offers a taste of classic Japanese flavors with meals ranging from teriyaki and tonkatsu to sushi and tempura.

*5. Hearty bowls of ramen, a Japanese noodle soup with a choice of broths and toppings, are served at Naoshima Ramen, a local favorite. The restaurant's delicious ramen and laid-back dining atmosphere are reasons for its success.

A lovely introduction to Naoshima's culinary scene, these informal dining alternatives and local eateries offer a taste of the island's fresh ingredients, traditional flavors, and cozy environment.

4.3 Coffee Shops and Cafés

In addition to its natural beauty and art museums, the island of Naoshima is home to a thriving cafe culture that appeals to a wide range of tastes. Naoshima's cafes provide a lovely diversion from touring the island's artistic treasures. They range from sophisticated coffee shops with views of the Seto Inland Sea to little cafes tucked away inside traditional Japanese residences.

***1. **Café Honmura:** Situated in the center of Honmura, the island's principal neighborhood, this establishment has a cozy, welcoming vibe. The cafe serves light meals, tea, and coffee that are all made with locally sourced, fresh ingredients. Whether you're looking for a peaceful afternoon respite or a morning pick-me-up, Cafe Honmura offers a comfortable environment in which to sip a cup of coffee and take in the peaceful atmosphere of Naoshima.

***2. Cafe Terrace:** Conveniently located close to the Honmura port, Cafe Terrace boasts a breathtaking view of the Seto Inland Sea, making it a charming setting for sipping coffee or a cool drink. The cafe serves a selection of light bites, teas, and coffees while offering a view of the tranquil waterways and passing boats.

****3. Located inside the Benesse House Museum, Apron Cafe offers a chic and practical place to stop in between viewing the museum's art exhibits. The cafe serves small meals, tea, coffee, and pastries that are all made with locally sourced, fresh ingredients. There are lots of possibilities to unwind and have a cup of coffee in the cafe's large seating area while taking in the creative atmosphere of the museum.

***4. **Nyaoshima Cafe:** Situated outside of Honmura, this cafe offers a distinctive fusion of contemporary coffee culture and traditional Japanese architecture. The cafe offers a selection of coffees, teas, and housemade treats in addition to exposed wooden beams and tatami flooring throughout. The cafe is well-liked by both locals and tourists due to its serene ambiance and blend of modern and traditional design elements.

*5. Shimacoya:** Adopting the idea of the "slow life," Shimacoya is a multi-use space that incorporates a variety store, a used bookshop, a cafe, and a guest house. The coffee, tea, and light snack options on the cafe's menu are all made with ingredients that are acquired locally. The cafe is a well-liked meeting place for both locals and tourists because of its laid-back vibe and diverse menu.

Naoshima's laid-back vibe and love of fine coffee are evident in these cafés and coffee shops.

4.4 Nightlife: Bars and Izakayas

After a day of touring the island's art museums and scenic areas, visitors can rest at one of Naoshima's many quaint bars or izakayas, which contribute to the town's peaceful ambiance at night. Naoshima's nightlife scene has something for everyone, whether you're looking for a classy bar with a view of the Seto Inland Sea or a local hangout place to enjoy a drink of sake.

***1. Honmura Bar: Tucked away in the Honmura neighborhood, this welcoming bar offers regional sake, shochu, and Japanese-inspired mixed drinks. Its cozy setting makes it a great place to hang out with friends or start a conversation with other tourists.

***2. Udon Honmura Izakaya: This vibrant izakaya, which is connected to the Udon Honmura restaurant, serves a broad assortment of Japanese tapas and drinks. It's a great place to try regional cuisine and take in the friendly izakaya ambiance.

****3. Naoshima Ramen Bar: **Located next to the Naoshima Ramen restaurant, this laid-back bar offers a casual setting for enjoying a drink and a bite to eat before or after indulging in a big bowl of ramen. It serves local beers, sake, and snacks.

***4. Benesse House Bar: ** Located inside the Benesse House Museum, this chic bar serves a variety of wines and cocktails and provides a view of the art installations. It's a perfect place to have a classy drink while surrounded by creative inspiration.

*5. Shimacoya Bar: ** Situated inside the Shimacoya complex, this laid-back bar is a favorite meeting place for both locals and tourists. It serves a variety of drinks and snacks in a laid-back ambiance.

Beyond these businesses, Naoshima has a few hidden gems to offer, like small bars nestled down side streets and traditional Japanese pubs called "kissaten." These hidden gems offer an authentic taste of the island's nightlife, a chance to interact with the locals and a glimpse into their world.

B. **After-hours Activities:**

Visitors can partake in a variety of nighttime activities in Naoshima in addition to sipping drinks at one of the bars or izakayas. These activities include:

1. * Taking in the lively ambiance and the traditional Japanese architecture while strolling through the lit-up streets of Honmura district.

2. Enjoy the peaceful atmosphere and stargazing beneath a clear night sky while unwinding on a beach or by the harbor.

3. * **Going to cultural events or performances,** such as music or dance performances in the traditional

Japanese style, which are held at different locations all year long.

4. * Holding discussions in izakayas or pubs with locals to learn more about their culture and way of life.

5. Shopping In Naoshima

5.1 Shops on Naoshima Island

Captivating island Naoshima, located in the Seto Inland Sea, has become a modern art and cultural hub, fusing creative expression with the tranquil natural beauty of the island. Its delightful selection of handicrafts, distinctive souvenirs, and artistic works are all part of its beautiful mix of art, nature, and local culture.

***1. Shop Benesse House: **
Both art lovers and those looking for mementos should make time to visit the Benesse House Shop, which is housed within the Benesse House Museum. The store sells products, art books, and stationery that are carefully chosen and drawn from the museum's collection as well as the creative spirit of the island.

***2. Honmura Naoshima Gallery: **
Located in the center of the Honmura area, the Naoshima Honmura Gallery features a selection of modern artwork

and handcrafted goods made by regional artists. The gallery offers a window into the artistic legacy and inventive spirit of the island through its changing exhibitions and one-of-a-kind pieces.

****3. Miyanoura Exhibition Rokku: **

Tucked away next to the Miyanoura ferry station, Miyanoura Gallery Rokku features a range of modern art, pottery, and regional handicrafts. The gallery offers a distinctive shopping experience, with its eclectic mix of artistic items reflecting the island's thriving arts culture.

***4. 695 Naoshima: **

Situated close to the Honmura harbor, the Naoshima 695 is a concept store that combines fashion, art, and lifestyle. The distinctive apparel, accessories, and home décor pieces in the store's carefully chosen assortment are all influenced by the island's scenic beauty and creative vibe.

*5. Honmura Udon:**

A local favorite, Udon Honmura serves you a variety of handcrafted udon noodles and related mementos. A glimpse of Naoshima's artistic and culinary heritage may be found in the store's handcrafted pottery, traditional Japanese tea towels, and savory udon packs.

Beyond these well-known stores, Naoshima has a wealth of undiscovered treasures strewn over its quaint alleyways and art galleries. Many distinctive findings encapsulate Naoshima's traditional charm and artistic energy, from small cafes serving artisanal pastries and local delicacies to local artists selling their handcrafted jewelry and pottery.

Shopping in Naoshima is more than just picking up trinkets and souvenirs; it's a chance to get a sense of the island's artistic culture and meet people. Every store reveals something new about Naoshima's artistic history, its relationship to the natural world, and the fervor of its residents through its thoughtfully chosen merchandise.

5.2 Regional Craft and Art Stores

Captivating island Naoshima, located in the Seto Inland Sea, has become a modern art and cultural hub, fusing creative expression with the tranquil natural beauty of the island. Its delightful selection of handicrafts, distinctive souvenirs, and artistic works are all part of its beautiful mix of art, nature, and local culture.

***1. Glass Naoshima Honmura: **
Located in the center of the Honmura area, Naoshima Honmura Glass displays the superb artistry of nearby glassblowers. Glassware ranging from practical tableware to delicate ornaments can be found in the shop's inventory. Each piece is handcrafted with great attention to detail and a passion for the art of glassblowing.

***2. Honmura Naoshima Pottery: **
The island's long pottery-making legacy is on display at Naoshima Honmura Pottery, which is situated in the quaint Honmura neighborhood. The array of ceramic

items in the shop ranges from modern artwork to traditional Japanese teacups; all are made with local clay and embody the distinct artistic culture of the island.

****3. Indigo Naoshima: **

Located close to the Naoshima ferry port, Naoshima Indigo specializes in textiles stained with indigo, a traditional Japanese art form with deep roots in the island's history. Each piece in the shop's inventory, which includes a range of indigo-dyed clothing, accessories, and home décor pieces, highlights the elegance and adaptability of this natural dye.

***4. Woodworks Naoshima: **

Situated in the serene environs of the Benesse Art Site Naoshima, Naoshima Woodworks features the artistry of regional woodturners. The wooden items in the shop's selection range from elaborate sculptures to useful bowls and utensils, all of which are expertly produced with a profound respect for the inherent beauty of wood.

*5. Paperworks Naoshima: **

Tucked down next to the Miyanoura ferry station, Naoshima Paperworks displays ancient Japanese papermaking techniques. A range of handcrafted paper goods, including ornamental stationery and delicate origami paper, are available in the shop; each item has a distinct handmade charm.

A glimpse into Naoshima's rich artistic legacy and the passion of its craftspeople may be found in these neighborhood art and craft stores. Made using regional materials and age-old methods, each item captures the spirit of the island's relationship to the natural world, love of fine workmanship, and commitment to upholding its creative heritage.

5.3 Keepsakes and Tributes

Captivating island Naoshima, located in the Seto Inland Sea, has become a modern art and cultural hub, fusing creative expression with the tranquil natural beauty of the island. Naoshima offers a beautiful selection of memories and souvenirs that encapsulate the essence of its artistic spirit, cultural history, and serene ambiance, in addition to its well-known art museums and natural attractions.

***1. Regional Handmade Items

-* **Ceramics:** The excellent collection of ceramics in Naoshima is a testament to the city's rich pottery-making legacy. These handcrafted works, which range from classic teacups and dinnerware to contemporary art pieces, highlight the artistry and workmanship of regional craftsmen.

-* **Glassware:** Renowned glassblowing studio Naoshima Honmura Glass creates elegant ornaments, useful tableware, and creative glass pieces that honor the island's aesthetic character and natural beauty.

-* **Indigo-Dyed Textiles:** Local textile studio Naoshima Indigo specializes in fashion, accessories, and home décor goods dyed with indigo. The elegance and adaptability of this traditional Japanese dye are exhibited in these handcrafted pieces.

***2. Souvenirs Inspired by Art**

-* **Art Books and Prints:** A variety of art books, prints, and posters inspired by the island's scenic surroundings and the works of well-known painters are available from the Benesse House Shop and other galleries on the island.

-* **Handmade Stationery:** A range of handmade stationery, from notebooks and greeting cards embellished with calligraphy and local art to traditional Japanese paper, is available from local shops and workshops.

-* **Unique Artistic Creations:** The creative energy of Naoshima is captured in a variety of handcrafted jewelry, sculptures, and decorative pieces that are among the many unique artistic mementos that have been inspired by the island's thriving art scene.

****3. Gourmet Treats**

-* **Local Tea and Sweets:** Naoshima provides a sense of the island's culinary traditions and natural flavors with a selection of teas grown locally and traditional Japanese sweets, like wagashi and mochi.

-* **Handmade Udon Noodles:** Visitors can reproduce the flavors of Naoshima's culinary scene in their kitchens with packages of Udon Honmura's signature handmade udon noodles, a local favorite.

-* **Olive Oil and Products:** Naoshima is well known for producing olive oil, and several stores sell bottles of the oil produced there, as well as soap made with olive oil and other items that encapsulate the island's agricultural past.

***4. Memorabilia of the Natural Beauty of Naoshima**

-* **Postcards and Photographs:** Preserve enduring memories of your island experience by capturing the beauty of Naoshima's scenery, art installations, and quaint villages in postcards and photos.

Handcrafted Maps & Guides: Handcrafted maps and guides to Naoshima, embellished with illustrations and creative touches, are available for purchase in local shops. These make for a distinctive memento of the island's layout and attractions.

-* **Locally Sourced Natural Materials:** Gather pebbles, driftwood, or seashells from Naoshima's beaches to create naturally sourced mementos that capture the peaceful vibe of the island.

These keepsakes and souvenirs act as concrete recollections of the alluring fusion of nature, culture, and art in Naoshima. Every item, whether it is made by regional craftspeople, features artwork by well-known artists or captures the natural beauty of the island, tells a tale about Naoshima's distinct character and the memories it makes for tourists.

5.4 Conventional Markets and Retail Avenues

Naoshima is well known for its modern art scene and art museums, but its quaint alleys and markets also provide a window into traditional Japanese culture. These lively places offer a fantastic chance to fully experience the island's regional cuisine, homemade handicrafts, and genuine vibe.

***1. Honmura Area: **

In the center of Naoshima, in the Honmura neighborhood, is a veritable gold mine of traditional stores and kiosks. A variety of stores selling local handicrafts, pottery, artisanal sweets, and fresh fruit may be found along narrow lanes flanked by wooden buildings and stone walkways. The laid-back vibe and friendly locals encourage strolls and impromptu explorations.

***2. Area of Miyanoura Ferry Terminal: **

The retail experiences in the vicinity of the Miyanoura ferry station are a blend of conventional and contemporary. Chic boutiques, galleries, and intimate cafes are dotted among the local stores that sell fresh seafood, regional specialties, and souvenirs. The bustling ambiance of the neighborhood is enhanced by the ferry terminal's dynamic energy.

****3. Area of Benesse House: **

In addition to the famous Benesse House Museum, there are several galleries and stores with an artistic flair in the Benesse House neighborhood. These businesses combine art appreciation with souvenir buying by offering a carefully chosen assortment of art books, prints, handcrafted stationery, and one-of-a-kind artistic creations.

***4. Honmura Udon:**

In the Honmura district, Udon Honmura is a well-known udon restaurant that doubles as a neighborhood market. A taste of Naoshima's culinary traditions is available to visitors through the purchase of freshly prepared udon noodles, regionally grown veggies, and traditional Japanese seasonings.

*5. Market for Farmers on Naoshima Island: **
The weekly Naoshima Island Farmers Market highlights the island's abundant agricultural produce. Fresh produce, jams, pickles, and other treats prepared by local farmers are brought, offering a chance to mingle with the islanders and enjoy the tastes of Naoshima.

Discovering Naoshima's traditional markets and retail avenues is about more than just shopping for mementos and sampling local fare—it's about absorbing the island's genuine culture, admiring the artistry of regional craftspeople, and feeling a connection to the friendly locals.

6. Top Must-visit Attractions in Naoshima

6.1 Museum of Chichu Art

Perched on a mountaintop with a view of the Seto Inland Sea, the Chichu Art Museum is both a haven for art lovers and a masterwork of architecture. Renowned architect Tadao Ando created the museum, which blends in well with the surrounding environment to create a peaceful interaction between art and nature.

Soichiro Fukutake has meticulously chosen the museum's collection, which includes pieces by well-known artists like Walter De Maria, James Turrell, and Claude Monet. Visitors can thoroughly immerse themselves in the creative expressions of each artwork thanks to the museum's architecture, which features a basic design and natural lighting.

The Chichu Art Museum's highlights:

-* **Claude Monet's Water Lilies:** An oval-shaped exhibit housing several Monet paintings serves as the focal point of the museum. Visitors may fully appreciate the delicate variations of color and light in Monet's masterpieces thanks to the immersive atmosphere.

-* **James Turrell's Blue Planet Sky:** Take in a captivating display of color and light with this site-specific work by the artist. Upon entering the dimly lit chamber, guests' eyes gradually acclimate to the large expanse of blue light that permeates the space, giving the impression of endless space and peace.

-* **Walter De Maria's Time and Space of Stones:** Set on a concrete plaza, this outdoor sculpture by Walter De Maria is made up of 133 black stones arranged in a grid. The piece's austere simplicity begs reflection on space, time, and the interaction between manmade and natural elements.

The Chichu Art Museum is proof of the ability of art to arouse strong emotions and transcend boundaries. Its well-balanced fusion of architecture, art, and landscape makes it a must-see location for art lovers and vacationers looking for a thought-provoking and life-changing experience.

6.2 Benesse House Museum

Situated on Naoshima Island, the expansive Benesse House Museum is a singularly compelling amalgam of art, architecture, and the surrounding landscape. The museum's Tadao Ando-designed structures harmoniously converse with the surrounding environment while blending into the island's topography.

The collection of the Benesse House Museum includes a wide variety of modern artwork, including paintings, sculptures, and installations by well-known creators like Bruce Nauman, Donald Judd, and Lee Ufan. Surrounded by the serene beauty of Naoshima's natural surroundings, visitors can engage in a meditative and immersive encounter with these artworks thanks to the museum's unique setting.

Features of the Museum at Benesse House:

-* **Lee Ufan's Circle of Relations:** A circular stone sculpture set inside a concrete plaza with a view of the Seto Inland Sea is the centerpiece of this site-specific installation by Lee Ufan. The piece encourages reflection on the connections between things, areas, and the natural world.

-* **Donald Judd's Untitled:** This minimalist sculpture by Donald Judd is made up of four galvanized steel rectangular boxes that are lined up along a hallway. The piece's industrial materials and stark simplicity subvert preconceived ideas about sculpture and compel viewers to think critically about the connection between materiality, form, and space.

-* **Bruce Nauman's 100 Live & Unseen Spirits:** In this video installation, 100 faces are projected one on top of the other onto different monitors. The faces talk together in real-time, becoming a cacophony of voices that delve into themes of communication, identity, and the essence of the self.

Surrounded by the tranquil serenity of Naoshima's natural surroundings, visitors can immerse themselves in modern art at the Benesse House Museum, providing a singular and transforming experience. It is a must-visit location for art fans and tourists looking for a harmonious fusion of art, architecture, and nature.

6.3 Museum of Lee Ufan

Located on Naoshima Island, the Lee Ufan Museum honors the artistic creations and life philosophy of well-known modern Korean artist Lee Ufan. Tadao Ando created the museum's minimalist building, which creates a peaceful environment for admiring Ufan's somber and thought-provoking pieces.

A wide variety of Ufan's artwork, including paintings, sculptures, and installations, are on display in the museum's collection. In addition to his paintings, which have an air of peace and harmony, the artist explores relationships between things, space, and the natural world in his minimalist sculptures and site-specific installations.

The Lee Ufan Museum's Highlights:

-* **"Relatum" series:** This body of work consists of sculptures with basic geometric shapes organized about their environment. These shapes are frequently composed of stone or wood. The pieces encourage reflection on harmony, balance, and the interaction between the natural world and human interference.

-* **"Circle of Relations"** (1992): Stone sculpture set on a concrete plaza with a view of the Seto Inland Sea is the centerpiece of this site-specific project. The piece encourages reflection on how things, space, and the viewer's perception interact.

-* **"In the Silence of the Stone"** (2008): This series of paintings conveys a sense of peace and nothingness through delicate ink brushstrokes on rice paper. The pieces induce a meditative state and encourage reflection on the passing of time and the meaning of life.

A singular chance to explore the thoughts and artistic expression of one of the most significant modern artists of our time is offered by the Lee Ufan Museum. The experience of Ufan's thought-provoking artworks is enhanced by the introspective mood created by its tranquil surroundings and minimalist design.

6.4 Art House Project

An amazing project on Naoshima Island called the Art House Project turns run-down homes into distinctive places for art and gathering places for the locals. Renowned artists and architects have worked together to restore these buildings, bringing the island's history to life and producing a vibrant and captivating art experience.

Every Art House Project location presents a unique artistic vision that embodies the spirit of cooperation among local artists, architects, and community members. By interacting with locals, taking part in workshops, and exploring installations, visitors can have a better understanding of the island's creative culture.

The Art House Project's Highlights:

-* **Gochi-So House:** Remodeled by Shinro Ohtake, this former restaurant now holds a collection of modern art and sponsors cultural events, offering a lively setting for creative expression and community involvement.

-* **Haisha:** Remodeled by SANAA, this old schoolhouse boasts modern art collections and minimalist design, harmonically combining art and education.

-* **Minami-Hondo:** Redesigned by Tadao Ando, this former community center offers a distinctive fusion of art and cultural heritage with several interconnected areas showcasing traditional Japanese architecture and contemporary art.

The Art House Project is evidence of the ability of art to inspire creativity and regenerate local communities. The project has improved the cultural landscape of the island and encouraged interaction and connection among locals and visitors by converting dilapidated buildings into colorful art venues.

6.5 Naoshima Bath

The relaxing and genuine Japanese bathing experience provided by the Naoshima Bath is available to visitors who are nestled in the peaceful environs of Naoshima Island. Renowned architect Tadao Ando created this one-of-a-kind public bathhouse that harmoniously combines architecture, nature, and wellness with the island's natural setting.

With its use of exposed concrete and natural light, the bathhouse's austere design captures Ando's distinct aesthetic and environmental consciousness. With its indoor and outdoor pools, the bathhouse lets guests take advantage of traditional Japanese bathing's healing properties while taking in Naoshima's scenic surroundings.

Naoshima Bath Highlights:

-* **Outdoor Bath with Panoramic Views:** Guests can unwind and rejuvenate themselves while soaking in the mineral-rich waters of the bathhouse's outdoor pool, which offers stunning views of the Seto Inland Sea.

-* **Authentic Japanese Bathing Ritual:** The bathhouse invites guests to cleanse and purify their bodies before submerging them in the hot water, by traditional Japanese bathing rituals.

-* **Therapeutic Benefits of Mineral Waters:** The natural mineral waters found in the bathhouse are well-known for their therapeutic qualities, which include enhancing circulation, relieving muscle tension, and encouraging relaxation.

-* **Harmonic Blend of Architecture and Nature:** Ando's sparse architecture creates a tranquil and harmonious setting by blending the bathhouse into the surrounding natural setting.

6.6 Ando Museum

Located on the island of Naoshima, the Ando Museum honors the architectural philosophy and body of work of well-known Japanese architect Tadao Ando. Ando designed the museum, which features his full-scale replicas, drawings, and architectural models. It offers a comprehensive look into his artistic vision and creative process.

The collection of the museum includes a thorough overview of Ando's architectural endeavors, ranging from his early creations to his globally acclaimed masterworks. Viewers can learn about Ando's design philosophies, his use of organic materials, and his dedication to making environmentally friendly settings.

Key Features of the Ando Museum:

-* **Architectural Models and Drawings:** A variety of Ando's architectural models are on display in the museum, ranging from his earliest sketches to meticulous reproductions of his most famous buildings.

-* **Full-Scale copies:** The museum showcases full-scale copies of some of Ando's most well-known pieces, giving visitors a close-up look at the architectural elements and spatial linkages.

-* **A deeper knowledge of Ando's creative process, his concept of "architecture as a space of silence," and his dedication to fostering harmonious relationships between architecture and nature are all made possible by visiting the museum.

-* **Interactive Displays and Multimedia Experiences:** To improve the visiting experience and realize Ando's architectural vision, the museum makes use of interactive displays and multimedia presentations.

One of the most significant architects of our time, Tadao Ando, left behind an enduring legacy, which is demonstrated by the Ando Museum. The museum offers an immersive and informative experience that inspires and enlightens visitors about the potential of architecture to shape spaces, enhance lives, and connect with the natural world by presenting architectural models, sketches, and full-scale replicas.

6.7 Teshima Island's Teshima Art Museum

Perched on the peaceful island of Teshima, the Teshima Art Museum is a haven for modern art as well as a masterwork of architecture. The museum's teardrop-shaped building, designed by famed architect Tadao Ando, harmoniously intertwines art and environment by blending into the island's natural surroundings.

The permanent exhibit "Matrix" by artist Rei Naito is the focal point of the museum. This site-specific installation turns the museum's interior into a contemplative, immersive area with its network of water channels and concrete walls. Wandering through the labyrinthine building, visitors can reflect on the relationship between human presence and the natural environment while taking in the interplay of light and shadow, water and sound.

Teshima Art Museum Highlights:

-* **Rei Naito's "Matrix" installation:** This immersive piece of art uses music, light, and water to create a transforming sensory experience that invites reflection on the link between human presence and the natural world.

-* **Harmonic Architecture by Tadao Ando:** Tadao Ando's teardrop-shaped museum building harmoniously blends into the island's natural surroundings, fostering a conversation between art and environment.

-* **Calm Island Setting:** The museum's setting on the peaceful island of Teshima contributes to a calm and reflective ambiance that heightens the experience of appreciating art.

-* **Educational Programs and Workshops:** The museum provides chances for a more in-depth understanding of modern art and the creative process through a range of educational programs and workshops.

6.8 Miyanoura Gallery 6 (MG6)

Situated on Naoshima Island, Miyanoura Gallery 6 (MG6) is a contemporary art gallery showcasing a wide variety of exhibitions, performances, and educational programs. The inventive and thought-provoking artworks are presented against a neutral backdrop created by Tadao Ando's minimalist architecture for the gallery.

The shows at MG6 showcase the creations of both seasoned and up-and-coming artists from across the globe, encompassing a diverse array of subjects and media. The gallery is a thriving center for modern art in the Setouchi region because of its dedication to encouraging experimentation and conversation.

Miyanoura Gallery 6 (MG6) Highlights:

-* **Varieties of Exhibitions:** MG6 presents a vibrant and captivating exhibition of contemporary art, ranging from painting and sculpture to installation and performance art.

-* **Minimalist Architecture by Tadao Ando:** Tadao Ando created the gallery's minimalist architecture, which draws attention to the artworks and creates a calm, meditative environment for appreciating art.

-* **Educational Programs and Workshops:** MG6 provides chances for more in-depth interaction with modern art and the creative process through a range of educational programs and workshops.

-* **Community Engagement Initiatives:** Through seminars, events, and partnerships, the gallery actively engages the local community, promoting a thriving Naoshima Island art scene.

In the center of Naoshima's art scene, Miyanoura Gallery 6 (MG6) provides a vibrant and enlightening experience for those looking to interact with the local community, immerse themselves in the transforming power of art, or engage with the creative energy of up-and-coming artists.

6.9 Honmura Area

The center of the island's art scene is the Honmura area, which is tucked away within Naoshima Island's bucolic surroundings. The bustling array of art galleries, museums, and contemporary artworks can be found in this quaint neighborhood, which is defined by its tiny lanes dotted with traditional Japanese residences and stone walks.

The district's many art spaces, each showcasing distinctive exhibitions, performances, and creative initiatives are a testament to its rich cultural past and artistic vitality. Wandering through the quaint alleyways, visitors can find hidden treasures and immerse themselves in the range of artistic expressions that characterize Naoshima.

The Honmura Area's Highlights:

-* **Benesse House:** This well-known museum complex, created by Tadao Ando, features a peaceful environment for appreciating art while housing a collection of contemporary works.

-* **Lee Ufan Museum:** This museum features minimalist sculptures and reflective paintings of well-known Korean artist Lee Ufan.

-* **Chichu Art Museum:** With a collection of Western art that includes pieces by Claude Monet and James Turrell, this museum is perched on a mountaintop overlooking the Seto Inland Sea.

-* **Art House Project:** This unique project revives the district's history while promoting creativity by converting abandoned houses into art spaces and community gathering places.

-* **Local Art Galleries and Shops:** Honmura is lined with numerous tiny art galleries and shops that sell a wide variety of crafts, artworks, and mementos.

The Honmura area is a vibrant community where art and daily life coexist harmoniously rather than just being a collection of art venues. In addition to exploring traditional crafts and interacting with local artists, visitors can enjoy the kind of hospitality that embodies Naoshima's distinct charm.

6.10 Naoshima Art Setouchi Triennale

The stunning international art festival Naoshima Art Setouchi Triennale turns the neighboring Setouchi region and Naoshima Island into a lively and energetic center of the arts. The festival, which takes place every three years, features a wide variety of contemporary art installations, exhibitions, and performances that turn unanticipated locations like ferry terminals, abandoned buildings, and natural settings into immersive artistic experiences.

The goals of the Naoshima Art Setouchi Triennale are to promote contemporary art appreciation in a distinctive and approachable manner, encourage cultural interaction, and rejuvenate communities. In addition to encouraging people to interact with art in novel and surprising ways, the festival also supports the sustainable development of the area by making use of pre-existing structures and incorporating art into daily life.

Highlights of the Setouchi Triennale of Naoshima Art:

-* **Site-Specific Art Installations:** Based on the natural beauty, cultural legacy, and architectural landscape of Naoshima and the Setouchi region, artists from all over the world create site-specific installations.

-* **Diverse Range of Art Forms:** The festival offers guests a full and captivating experience by showcasing a diverse range of art forms, such as painting, sculpture, installation, performance art, and sound art.

-* **Community Engagement Initiatives:** Through partnerships, educational initiatives, and workshops, the festival actively involves the local community, promoting a sense of pride and ownership in the area's artistic character.

-* **Revitalization of Abandoned Spaces:** The festival gives dilapidated buildings and undeveloped areas a new lease on life by transforming them into temporary art venues. This helps to revitalize the area.

-* **Accessibility and Inclusiveness:** The festival offers a range of activities and initiatives that cater to varied audiences, including children, families, and those with disabilities, to make art accessible to everyone.

The Naoshima Art Setouchi Triennale is evidence of the ability of art to inspire creativity, break down barriers, and unite communities. Its dedication to creativity, sustainability, and community involvement has helped the area's economic and cultural revival while also making it a globally renowned destination for the arts.

7. Transportation And Costs In Naoshima

7.1 How to Travel to Naoshima

Explore the beautiful island of Naoshima in the Seto Inland Sea; it's a refuge for nature lovers and art fans alike. It has become a well-liked travel destination for people all over the world because of its distinctive fusion of modern art installations, traditional Japanese architecture, and breathtaking natural beauty.

7.1.1. Ferry

The most practical and picturesque method to go to Naoshima is by ferry. Numerous ferry services are available from several ports in the Setouchi area, such as Takamatsu, Uno, and Okayama.

The closest port to Naoshima is Uno, and the boat voyage from there takes around 20 minutes and gives stunning views of the Seto Inland Sea. Once in

Naoshima, it's simple to get around the island by bus, bicycle, or foot, taking in the art attractions.

**Ferry Companies **

* Shikokukisen.com/en/instant/ - Is the Uno Port.
* Benesse House Accessible: at https://benesse-artsite.jp/en/

7.1.2 By Bus and Train

Trains and buses are other ways to get to Naoshima for those coming from further out. You can travel to Okayama Station via the Shinkansen bullet train from major cities such as Osaka, Kyoto, and Hiroshima. Take the Uno Line train from Okayama Station to Uno Station, where you can change to a ferry to Naoshima.

Advice on Transportation

Buy ferry tickets in advance during busy times of the year to guarantee availability and avoid long lines.

-* **Verify ferry timetables thoroughly**; they are subject to seasonal or meteorological changes.

-* To prevent missing connections, **Allow adequate time for transfers** between trains and boats.

-* **Take into account getting a Naoshima Art Pass**; this saves you money on ferry tickets, local transportation, and museum entry.

-* **Hiring a bike** is a well-liked and practical method to see the little island of Naoshima.

-* **Delight in the scenic voyage** and enjoy the breathtaking views of the Seto Inland Sea.

7.2 How to Navigate Naoshima

There are several ways to go to Naoshima, an enthralling island in the Seto Inland Sea so that tourists can discover its scenic surroundings, artistic sites, and quaint little towns. Naoshima offers options for everyone's taste, whether it is public transportation for its ease or cycling at a more leisurely pace.

7.2.1 Electric and Rental Bicycles

Renting an electric bike or bicycle is a well-liked and practical way to navigate the small island of Naoshima. Riding a bicycle is a pleasant and relaxed way to discover the island's museums, galleries, and independent stores because of its smooth roads and mild inclines. For those who wish to cover more ground or take on some of the steeper inclines, electric bikes provide an extra push.

Reservation Sites

Bicycle rental shops may be found all across the Honmura district, which is the center of Naoshima's art scene, as well as close to the ferry terminals. These stores sell a range of bicycle models, such as tandem bikes for families or couples, electric bikes, and regular bicycles.

Rates for Rent

Bicycle rentals usually cost between ¥500 and ¥1,000 per day, whereas electric bike rentals can run between ¥1,500 and ¥2,000 per day. Discounts for multi-day rentals are also frequently offered by rental stores.

7.2.2 Public Transport

Additionally, Naoshima features a compact yet practical public transit network that connects the city's major sights and communities. A local bus travels through the Honmura area, home to many of the art institutions, on its route from Miyanoura Ferry Terminal to Tsutsuji-so. A free shuttle bus runs between Tsutsuji-so and Benesse House and the Lee Ufan Museum.

A Guide to Public Transportation

-* **Make sure you schedule your travel in advance** so you can catch the right busses and shuttle bus connections.

-* **Allow enough time to travel** between destinations because bus frequencies can be restricted.

-* If you intend to do more exploring, **Think about renting a bicycle for greater flexibility and convenience**.

-* **Delight in the picturesque bus rides** and enjoy the vistas of the villages and scenery of Naoshima.

7.3 Passes and Transportation Fees

The fascinating island of Naoshima in Japan's Setouchi area provides a singular fusion of culture, art, and scenic beauty. It's crucial to arrange your transportation and comprehend the many price options and passes available if you want to fully enjoy the island's many attractions.

Costs of Transportation

1. * **Ferry Tickets:** One-way ferry tickets cost between ¥1,000 and ¥2,000 from Okayama or Uno to Naoshima.

2. * **Bicycle Rentals:** The cost of renting a bicycle normally runs between ¥500 and ¥1,000 per day, whereas the cost of renting an electric bike can be between ¥1,500 and ¥2,000 per day.

3. * **Public Transportation:** The shuttle bus is free, but local bus fares are ¥100 for adults and ¥50 for children.

4. * **Taxi Fees:** Starting at roughly ¥500, taxi costs are metered.

Passes for Transportation

Many savings and advantages are available with the Naoshima Art Pass, such as discounted ferry tickets, discounted transit in Naoshima, and free entry to art museums. The pass costs between ¥1,500 and ¥3,900 and is offered in one-, two-, and three-day variations.

8. Accommodation & Price Ranges for Naoshima

8.1 Hotel & Museum Benesse House

Renowned Japanese architect Tadao Ando created the Benesse House Museum and Hotel, a distinctive and motivational place to stay on Naoshima Island. This amazing building offers guests an immersive experience in a tranquil natural setting by skillfully fusing art, architecture, and hospitality.

A. **Lodging Alternatives**

Benesse House offers a range of lodging choices to accommodate various tastes and price ranges. There are four different venues available to guests, each with its special charm and personality:

1. * **Museum Deluxe Twin Rooms**: Situated on the second level of the Benesse House Museum, these airy

rooms have direct access to the museum's collection as well as breathtaking views of the Seto Inland Sea.

2. * **Oval:** Designed by Tadao Ando, this modern, minimalist structure has rooms that are fashioned like circles and offer expansive views of the sea.

3. * **Park:** Nestled in a peaceful park, these comfortable rooms provide a feeling of peace amid rich vegetation.

4. * **Beach:** Located close to the seaside, these laid-back yet cozy accommodations offer easy access to the sand and the soothing sounds of the sea.

B. **Eating Alternatives**

In addition to art and lodging, Benesse House provides a range of food alternatives. The Museum Restaurant offers a classy dining experience with an emphasis on regional, seasonal foods, and floor-to-ceiling windows that overlook the Seto Inland Sea. The Beach Café offers a laid-back environment to take in the views of the sea, while the Oval Café serves light fare and drinks in a more informal setting.

C. **Unique Attributes and Experiences**

More than just a place to sleep, a visit to Benesse House Museum and Hotel is an immersive experience that combines architecture, art, and nature. After hours, visitors are free to peruse the museum's collection, take in the peace of the island's natural surroundings, and interact with the creative energy that permeates the space.

D. **Price Ranges**

The cost of lodging at Benesse House Museum and Hotel varies according to the type of room chosen, the time of year, and the duration of stay. However, as a general rule of thumb, a double occupancy room will cost you between ¥25,000 and ¥60,000 each night.

8.2 Additional Distinctive Lodging Choices

Beyond the well-known Benesse House Museum and Hotel, Naoshima Island has a range of distinctive and quaint lodging choices to fit a range of tastes and price ranges. These lodgings offer the chance to take in the serene ambiance of the island, encounter customary Japanese kindness, and stumble across undiscovered treasures on the route.

***1. Honmura Terrace's minimalist architecture

Located in the center of Honmura, the hub of Naoshima's art scene, Honmura Terrace is a modern, minimalist hotel that blends in perfectly with the island's architectural landscape. Reputable architect Tadao Ando created the hotel, which has roomy rooms with tatami floors and huge windows framing tranquil views of the surrounding gardens.

***2. Historic Japanese Charm at Shishikura Guest House **

A taste of traditional hospitality is offered by Guest House Shishikura to guests looking for an authentic Japanese experience. The renovated Japanese house became a beautiful guesthouse with tatami rooms, shared bathrooms, and a peaceful garden location. Indulge in home-cooked meals made with regional products while experiencing the coziness and minimalism of Japanese culture.

****3. Calm Haven at Konbutei**

Perched on a hill with a view of the Seto Inland Sea, Konbutei provides a peaceful haven amidst the natural surroundings. This former seaweed processing facility has been converted into a distinctive guesthouse with large rooms that offer expansive views of the sea and an emphasis on ecological methods. Visitors can take part in traditional Japanese activities, eat meals that are sourced locally, and relax in the island's beautiful surroundings.

***4. Stay Inspired by Art at I&S Naoshima**

I&S Naoshima offers visitors who are passionate about art an immersive experience that blends lodging with art enjoyment. Housed in a former schoolhouse, this unusual hotel has modern art pieces throughout its common areas and guest rooms. Visitors can take part in art workshops, peruse the hotel's art collection, and take in the lively atmosphere filled with artistic expressions.

*5. Guest House Solare Offers Inexpensive Comfort**
Budget-conscious guests have a pleasant and reasonably priced lodging option in Guest House Solare. This contemporary guesthouse offers tidy, well-kept rooms, a communal kitchen, and a rooftop terrace overlooking the island's roofs. Visitors can take their time discovering the island's attractions and appreciate the practicality of being in the heart of Honmura.

*6. The Honmura-tei Guest House **
With its wooden architecture and tatami mat flooring, Guest House Honmura-tei, located in the center of the Honmura neighborhood, radiates a classic Japanese charm. A range of room options, including shared and

individual rooms with Western-style or tatami beds, are available at the guest house. A traditional Japanese breakfast is served to guests, who can then unwind in the communal spaces that are adorned with artwork and locally made crafts.

*7. The Island Residence**
Situated just a short stroll from the Miyanoura ferry station, The Island House provides modern, minimalist lodging. The guest house has rooms that are large and have floor-to-ceiling windows that let in a lot of natural light and offer breathtaking views of the Seto Inland Sea. Numerous facilities are available to visitors, such as a rooftop patio, a library, and a shared kitchen.

*8. Shiota Guest House **
Guest House Shiota, created by the well-known artist Setsuko Shiota, is a work of art unto itself. Shiota created pieces for the guest house, such as a room with red lines painted on the walls and another with wool threads everywhere. Visitors can interact with the artist's

creations and take in the distinctive ambiance of this out-of-the-ordinary lodging.

* **9. Naoshima Uchiumi **

Nestled in the peaceful surroundings of Naoshima, Uchiumi Naoshima provides a calm and private haven. The guest house offers traditional wooden furniture and simple Japanese-style rooms with tatami mat flooring. A shared bath that offers a peaceful bathing experience and is surrounded by nature is available to guests.

* **10. Tsujimoto's Naoshima Guest House **

The cozy and inviting Naoshima Guest House Tsujimoto is close to the Benesse House Museum. To accommodate varying tastes, the guest house offers comfortable rooms decorated in the Western style as well as traditional Japanese design. Indulge in a homemade breakfast and unwind in the cozy common areas.

These distinctive lodging choices on Naoshima Island offer guests a variety of experiences, from minimalist contemporary design to traditional Japanese hospitality, all blended with the calm natural beauty and art-centric environment of the island.

8.3 Reasonably Priced Lodging

There are several lodging choices available on the lovely island of Naoshima in the Seto Inland Sea to accommodate a range of tastes and price ranges. Even though the well-known Benesse House Museum and Hotel offers an opulent and artistic experience, there are plenty of affordable options that let guests enjoy the island's natural beauty and charm to the fullest without going over budget.

***1. Solare Guest House **
Guest House Solare is a well-liked option for tourists on a tight budget because it provides reasonably priced, spotless shared rooms. The guesthouse's central location in Honmura, Naoshima's major hamlet, makes it simple to visit the galleries, museums, and shops dedicated to the island's artistic culture. Additionally, Guest House

Solare offers a common kitchen so that visitors may cook for themselves and save money on dining out.

***2. Kominka Guest House **

At a reasonable price, Guest House Kominka gives a flavor of local culture in a refurbished farmhouse setting, allowing guests to enjoy a traditional Japanese experience. The guesthouse lets visitors experience the peace and simplicity of Japanese living with its tatami mat floors, shared bathrooms, and peaceful garden. In keeping with the traditional lodgings, Guest House Kominka offers a gastronomic experience that includes authentic Japanese cuisine.

****3. Hostel Naoshima **

A lively and communal lodging choice, Naoshima Hostel offers reasonably priced dorm-style accommodations. Access to the island's attractions is made simple by the hostel's handy position close to the ferry port. Naoshima Hostel offers spaces for socializing and unwinding, including a rooftop terrace with views of the neighborhood, a common kitchen, and a public lounge area.

***4. Minshuku Umi no Ie**

For a reasonable price, Minshuku Umi no Ie provides a warm and authentic Japanese bed and breakfast experience. The beachside minshuku offers tatami mat rooms, shared bathrooms, and a homemade breakfast made with regional products. The proprietor of the minshuku is kind and welcoming, and guests can appreciate the genuine charm of Japanese accommodation.

*5. The URA Naoshima Guest House **

The Guest House URA Naoshima provides reasonably priced lodging that is both contemporary and cozy. The guesthouse offers tidy, well-maintained accommodations for a comfortable stay, including individual rooms with communal bathrooms. Situated close to the ferry terminal and bus station, Guest House URA Naoshima offers an ideal position from which to explore the island.

Advice for Inexpensive Lodging

-* Reserve your lodging in advance to ensure the best deals and availability, particularly during busy times of the year.

If you're looking for a more affordable option, think about booking a room in a shared apartment or dorm.

-* Make use of shared spaces, such as communal kitchens, to make meals and save dining out costs.

-* Look outside of Honmura's main village to uncover hidden treasures with less expensive lodging.

-* To save on paying for a taxi or rental car, use the island's public transportation system and bicycles.

On Naoshima, inexpensive lodging options offer a cozy and cost-effective starting point for discovering the island's artistic, cultural, and scenic highlights. Visitors can still take advantage of the unique experiences

Naoshima has to offer without sacrificing comfort or convenience by opting for a more affordable choice.

8.4 Options for Housestays and Guesthouses

There are several lodging choices available on the lovely island of Naoshima in the Seto Inland Sea to accommodate a range of tastes and price ranges. In addition to lodging options such as hotels and hostels, Naoshima offers distinctive homestay and guesthouse experiences that let guests fully immerse themselves in the daily life and culture of the island.

A. **Residence Experience**

A homestay program that places you with a local host gives you a genuine, immersive introduction to Naoshima's customs and culture. Homestay hosts are enthusiastic about sharing their island home with visitors, giving them an inside look at daily life, customs, and language. Typical experiences include home-cooked dinners that offer a flavor of Naoshima's culinary customs and are made using seasonal, fresh ingredients.

B. **Experiencing the Guesthouse**

Compared to regular hotels, guesthouses offer a more laid-back and social atmosphere that encourages contact and a sense of community among visitors. typical spaces including lounge areas, kitchens, and gardens are typical to many guesthouses, providing opportunities for visitors to socialize, exchange tales, and take in the peaceful ambiance of the island. Guesthouses frequently organize cultural events, seminars, and outings that give visitors a chance to interact with the locals and take in the lively energy of Naoshima.

Guesthouse and Homestay Suggestions

Here are a few well-liked hotel and homestay choices in Naoshima:

1. * **Guest House Shishikura:** With tatami rooms, shared bathrooms, and a peaceful garden location, this traditional Japanese guesthouse offers a sense of the local way of life.

2. * **Minshuku Umi no Ie:** Cozy and pleasant, this minshuku serves homemade breakfast in a homey setting.

3. * **Guest House URA Naoshima:** Conveniently located close to the ferry station, this contemporary and cozy guesthouse offers private rooms.

4. * **Kominka Guest House Naoshima:** Remodeled with tatami mat floors, shared bathrooms, and a tranquil garden, this farmhouse offers a classic Japanese experience.

5. * **I&S Naoshima:** With modern art installations in both its common areas and guest rooms, this art-infused guesthouse blends lodging with a love of art.

8.5 Camping and Outside Lodging

The fascinating island of Naoshima in the Seto Inland Sea has a variety of housing choices, including an exceptional outdoor camping experience. Naoshima, surrounded by the peace of nature, offers a calm location where one can fully appreciate the natural beauty of the surroundings and have a memorable, rustic stay.

. **Rest Areas**

Naoshima has several official camping areas, each providing a unique experience among the island's scenic surroundings. These campgrounds offer a variety of facilities and services to suit different tastes and camping experience levels.

1. * **Naoshima Island Campground:** This campground offers a great setting with breathtaking views of the Seto Inland Sea, and it's close to the Benesse House Museum.

2. Located in the middle of a verdant forest, the **Tsutsuji-so Camping Ground** offers a peaceful setting near the Tsutsuji-so artworks.

3. * **Gokuraku-to Island Camping Site:** This isolated island, which is reachable by ferry from Naoshima, provides a private camping experience in unspoiled natural surroundings.

B. **Ambient Housing Options**

In addition to conventional camping, Naoshima provides distinctive outdoor lodging choices that blend the conveniences of contemporary hotel with the peace of the outdoors. These choices preserve the spirit of outdoor living while offering a more planned and practical camping experience.

1. * **Glamping Naoshima:** This opulent glamping destination provides fully furnished tents with cozy mattresses, electricity, and the use of shared restrooms and showers.

2. * **Setouchi Natural Retreat Glamping:** Offering expansive views and a peaceful haven amidst nature, this glamping location is perched on a mountaintop overlooking the Seto Inland Sea.

3. * **Shima Kaze Terrace:** This distinctive lodging choice offers a fusion of indoor and outdoor life with a mix of tent-style accommodations and traditional Japanese tatami rooms.

The advantages of camping and staying outside

-* **Immersion in Nature:** Away from the rush of daily life, camping, and outdoor lodging offer the chance to completely appreciate the beauty of Naoshima's natural surroundings.

-* **Rustic and Memorable Experience:** Sleeping beneath the stars and becoming in tune with the island's organic rhythms provide a rustic and distinctive experience that will stay with you forever.

-* **Budget-Friendly Alternatives:** Travelers on a tight budget may find camping and other outdoor lodging to be more economical than standard motels.

-* **Sustainability and low Impact:** In keeping with Naoshima's dedication to protecting its natural beauty, these solutions support sustainability and low environmental impact.

Enjoy the ease of living outside, take in the serene beauty of the island, and make lifelong memories beneath Naoshima's starry skies.

9. Outdoor Activities In Naoshima

9.1 Coastal Activities & Beaches

The fascinating island of Naoshima in the Setouchi Sea is a remarkable fusion of culture, art, and scenic beauty. Its tranquil shoreline, which is peppered with quiet coves and sandy beaches, offers a refuge for leisure, discovery, and a range of water sports.

1. **Beaches for Relaxation and Unwinding**

The beaches of Naoshima are a peaceful haven, with perfect places to take in the sun, savor the mild sea wind, and listen to the quiet sounds of the waves.

1. * **Honmura Beach**: This quaint little beach is ideal for a stroll along the shoreline or a quick swim. It is situated in the center of the Honmura neighborhood.

2. * **Okunohama Beach:** Tucked away in a quiet cove, this immaculate beach provides a peaceful

environment for swimming, tanning, and taking in the expansive views of the Seto Inland Sea.

3. * **Goshuku Beach**: This charming beach offers an exquisite setting for a tranquil getaway. It is well-known for its unusual rock formations and glistening seas.

B. **Adventure and Exploration via Coastal Activities**

Naoshima's shoreline offers a range of activities that suit adventurous souls and those looking for a more active experience, in addition to sunbathing and relaxation.

1. * **Kayaking and Stand-Up Paddleboarding:** Paddle around the calm seas to discover the island's secret coves and isolated inlets and take in the quiet coastline beauty from a different angle.

2. * **Snorkeling and Diving:** Explore Naoshima's underwater world by snorkeling or diving its crystal-clear waters, where you'll come across a diverse

range of marine life surrounded by rocky formations and coral reefs.

3. * **Island Hopping:** Take a ferry to nearby islands to discover their distinctive landscapes, art installations, and quaint settlements, such as Gokuraku-to and Inujima.

A Guide to Coastal Activities and Beaches

-* **Respect the Natural Environment**: Take care to dispose of rubbish appropriately, leave no trace, and show consideration for coastal habitats and marine life.

-* **Select the Appropriate Time of Day:** Go to beaches in the morning or late afternoon to escape the busiest times and take in the peace of the area.

-* **Pack Appropriate Gear:** For sunbathing and coastal activities, bring sunscreen, a hat, sunglasses, and appropriate swimwear.

-* **Be Aware of Water Conditions:** Only swim in locations marked by tide charts and weather predictions.

-* **Explore and Find Hidden Gems:** For a more solitary and tranquil experience, venture beyond the popular beaches to find hidden coves and locations.

9.2 Routes for Bicycling and Riding

Bicycling is a delightful and practical way to discover Naoshima, an enthralling island in the Setouchi Sea, with its museums, art installations, and picturesque scenery. The island is a great place for relaxing rides and exciting adventures because of its gentle hills, well-maintained roads, and designated bike routes.

A. **Trails for Art Lovers on cycling routes**

Experience the vibrant art scene of Naoshima by riding these routes, which link famous art installations and institutions:

1. * **Honmura Art Cycle Route:** Visit the Benesse House Museum, the Naoshima Museum, and several art galleries and installations as you cycle through the center of Honmura, the major village on Naoshima.

2. * **Tsutsuji-so Art Cycle Route:** Take a picturesque ride along the Tsutsuji-so Art Cycle Route, which passes by several other outdoor art projects among lush foliage, including the well-known red pumpkin sculpture.

3. * **Benesse Art Cycle Route:** Take this route around the Benesse House complex to see the stunning architecture and Tadao Ando-designed art installations.

B. **Roads for Cyclists Who Love Nature**

Take in the natural beauty of Naoshima by riding these routes, which highlight the island's various landscapes:

1. * **Coastal Cycle Route:** Enjoy the cool coastal breeze while cycling along this route, which offers

breathtaking views of the Seto Inland Sea as well as quiet coves and quaint harbors.

2. * **Island Loop Cycle Route:** Take on a challenge by cycling the island's circumference on the lengthier, more difficult Island Loop Cycle Route, which offers breathtaking views and undiscovered treasures along the way.

3. * **Mountain Bike Trail:** Set off on an exciting bike ride through the verdant forests of the island and climb picturesque vistas along the Mountain Bike Trail.

Guides for Riding a Bike or Cycling on Naoshima

-* **Rent a Bike:** There are conveniently accessible bike rental outlets all across the Honmura district and close to the ferry terminals.

-* **Follow Designated riding lanes:** To ensure efficient and safe navigation, stick to the clearly defined riding lanes.

-* **Be Aware of Pedestrians:** Be considerate of other drivers and yield to pedestrians on the road, particularly in congested places.

-* **Respect the Environment:** To maintain the island's natural beauty, refrain from littering and dispose of waste correctly.

-* **Enjoy the Ride:** Go slowly, appreciate the surroundings, and let yourself be taken aback by surprising revelations along the journey.

9.3 Nature Walks and Hiking Trails

The captivating island Naoshima in the Setouchi Sea provides a calm retreat into the embrace of nature. Naoshima is known for its renowned art scene and quaint villages, but it's also home to a vast network of hiking trails and nature hikes that reveal the island's undiscovered beauty and offer tranquil exploring opportunities.

A. **Trails for Hiking that Offer Stunning Views and Difficult Ascents**

Hiking routes in Naoshima offer both challenge and reward, as they lead to stunning overlooks and allow you to fully experience the island's natural splendor.

1.* **Honmura walk:** This moderately strenuous walk winds through the center of Honmura, the major hamlet, before climbing to a viewpoint point with expansive views of the surrounding islands and the Seto Inland Sea.

2. * **Tsutsuji-so walk:** This lovely walk meanders through verdant vegetation, circling the famous red pumpkin sculpture and ending at a calm vantage point with a view of the Tsutsuji-so art site.

3. * **Gokuraku-to Trail:** Take on a strenuous climb to the top of Gokuraku-to, a nearby island, with

unmatched views of the far-off mountains, the Seto Inland Sea, and Naoshima.

B. **Nature Walks for Calm and Relaxation**

Take a stroll around Naoshima's serene natural surroundings to find comfort and calm away from the daily grind:

1.* * * Coastal Walk: Breathe in the clean sea air and take in the tranquil sounds of the waves lapping against the shore as you stroll around the island's coastline.

2. * **Forest Walk:** Take a stroll into the peaceful forests of Naoshima, where you may discover the island's varied flora and animals by following meandering paths among towering trees.

3. * **Rice Paddy Walk** Observe the beauty of rural life and the island's rich agricultural legacy as you meander through the tranquil settings of Naoshima's rice paddies.

9.4 Tour by Kayaking

Take a guided kayaking tour to explore the island's unique marine environment and uncover its hidden gems:

1. * **Guided Kayaking Tour of Honmura Coast:** Paddle past traditional Japanese homes, artwork, and quiet coves as you explore the scenic coastline of Honmura, the main village on Naoshima.

2. **Kayaking Tour to Inujima Island:** Take a kayak tour to the nearby island of Inujima, which is well-known for its distinctive architecture and art installations. Along the way, take in the expansive vistas of the Seto Inland Sea.

3. * **Gokuraku-to Island Kayaking Tour:** Take a kayak tour to discover the remote beauty of Gokuraku-to Island, renowned for its unspoiled natural landscapes and peaceful environment. Savor the peace of the surrounding seas.

Discovering hidden gems, floating across the calm waters, and exploring the island's shoreline are all made possible by kayaking on Naoshima, which offers an exciting and rejuvenating experience.

10. Events & Festivals in Naoshima

10.1 The Setouchi Triennial of Art

Every three years, Naoshima and adjacent islands in the Seto Inland Sea host the massive worldwide Setouchi Triennale Art Festival. The festival presents performances and installations of modern art, converting the islands into a thriving center for artistic expression and cross-cultural interaction.

A. **Setouchi Triennale Art Festival History and Overview**

To revive the Seto Inland Sea region, which had suffered economic collapse as a result of Japan's deindustrialization, the Setouchi Triennale Art Festival was first staged in 2000. Since then, the festival has grown into a significant cultural occasion that draws tourists from all over the world to witness the original and cutting-edge performances and artworks that take place on the islands.

B. **Setouchi Triennale Art Festival Highlights**

The Setouchi Triennale Art Festival is renowned for its wide selection of art installations, many of which are site-specific and make use of the island's exceptional architectural and natural beauty. Among the most prominent installations to date have been:

1. * **The Red Pumpkin:** On the shore at Goshuku Island, there is a sizable red pumpkin sculpture created by Yayoi Kusama.

2. * **The House of Water:** A glass-walled living room with a view of the Seto Inland Sea and a water patio characterize this minimalist concrete home designed by Tadao Ando.

3. * **The Chichu Art Museum:** A collection of modern art, including pieces by Monet, Rodin, and James Turrell, is housed in this Tadao Ando-designed museum.

The Setouchi Triennale Art Festival offers a range of performances, seminars, and educational programs in addition to art installations. The festival gives up-and-coming performers and artists a stage on which to present their work, and it also gives the general audience a chance to interact meaningfully with modern art.

C. **Setouchi Triennale Art Festival Impact**

The Seto Inland Sea region has benefited greatly from the Setouchi Triennale Art Festival, which has revitalized the islands and drawn tourists from all over the world. In addition, the festival has helped to stimulate cross-cultural exchanges between Japan and other nations and revive the local economy.

D. **Organizing Your Setouchi Triennale Art Festival Visit**

Every third year, for three months in the spring and fall, Setouchi hosts the Setouchi Triennale Art Festival. A festival passport that grants entry to every art installation and performance is available for purchase by visitors. To aid tourists in exploring the islands, the festival also provides a range of transportation choices, such as buses, bicycles, and boats.

10.2 Celebrations and Festivals of Local Culture

In addition to the internationally recognized Setouchi Triennale Art Festival, Naoshima is home to other regional cultural festivals and events all year long that provide tourists with an insight into the island's vibrant local culture and rich traditions. By showcasing the island's distinctive history, delectable cuisine, and creative expressions, these events help visitors appreciate Naoshima's true appeal.

1. The Summer Festival in Naoshima

The lively Naoshima Summer Festival, which takes place every August, features music, dance, and traditional festivities. The streets are brought to life with vibrant decorations, upbeat music, and the delicious smell of regional cuisine. A wide selection of regional cuisine and beverages can be sampled, as well as captivating fireworks displays and traditional Japanese dances.

2. **Harvest Festival of Honmura**

The Honmura Harvest Festival honors the abundance of the island's agricultural products in the fall. A vibrant market environment is created when farmers congregate to showcase their recently gathered fruits, vegetables, and other locally produced goods. In addition to purchasing fresh fruit and enjoying local specialties, visitors can take in traditional farmer's dances and performances.

3. **Festival of Gokuraku-to Island**

Every year in May, the lonely island of Gokuraku-to is transformed into a thriving center of the arts by the unique Gokuraku-to Island Festival. International artists get together to create transient art pieces that perfectly complement the island's unspoiled beauty. Discover hidden art jewels, stroll around the island's coves, and take in the peaceful ambiance amid artistic expression.

4. **Festival of Tsutsuji-so Art Site**

Held in the spring, the Tsutsuji-so Art Site Festival pairs art with nature against the magnificent backdrop of the island's azalea blooms. Wander around the vibrantly colored azalea-filled gardens, take in temporary art exhibits, and take in live musical performances. In addition, the festival offers seminars and traditional Japanese tea rituals, providing a sense of the local way of life and artistic talent.

5. **Festival of Winter Solstice**

Naoshima celebrates the Winter Solstice Festival on the shortest day of the year, a time for introspection, rebirth, and camaraderie. All across the island, bonfires are lighted, giving the winter sky a cozy glow. In addition to partaking in customs that represent purification and cleaning, guests can congregate around the bonfires and savor traditional Japanese cuisine and beverages.

A deeper understanding of the customs, values, and artistic manifestations of Naoshima can be gained by participating in local cultural events and festivities. These gatherings provide an opportunity to fully experience the spirit of the neighborhood, enjoy the delectable flavors of traditional Naoshima cuisine, and make enduring memories of the island's distinctive cultural legacy.

10.3 Live Events and Musical Shows

In addition to its well-known art scene and serene natural beauty, Naoshima has a thriving cultural scene. The island hosts a range of live music events and shows that highlight the island's wide range of artistic expressions and provide year-round entertainment for tourists. These events offer a unique chance to explore the island's rich cultural diversity and interact with local artists and performers. They range from concerts of modern music to traditional Japanese performances.

1. **Classic Japanese Instrumentals**

Traditional Japanese performances showcasing the island's deeply ingrained customs and artistic expressions bring Naoshima's cultural legacy to life. Visitors can experience the mesmerizing rhythms of Taiko drumming performances, where thunderous drum beats resonate through the air or witness the elegance of Noh theater, a highly stylized type of Japanese play. In addition, traditional Japanese dance performances like Kagura and Bon Odori provide an insight into the customs and folklore of the island.

2. **Concerts of Contemporary Music**

Naoshima offers a range of events featuring contemporary music, including jazz, classical, and other genres, for those who enjoy listening to music. Live music can be experienced in an immersive environment at the island's small venues, where events are frequently held against the backdrop of beautiful scenery and artworks. Discover the soulful melodies of classic Japanese instruments like the Koto and Shamisen, or listen to up-and-coming local musicians.

3. **Live Music and Performance Festivals**

The annual events in Naoshima, like the Honmura Harvest Festival and the Naoshima Summer Festival, honor regional customs while also providing an opportunity to see live acts. On outdoor stages, guests may take in exciting musical acts ranging from modern pop and rock bands to traditional Japanese folk music. The festivals provide a lively environment where art, music, and a sense of community come together.

4. **Separate Performance Locations**

The island's distinctive architectural buildings, such as the I&S Naoshima, and the Benesse House Museum, make unusual yet alluring settings for live music concerts. These areas combine art and sound design to provide a fully immersive experience that merges music and visual arts. To augment the whole cultural experience, visitors can take in performances amid modern art pieces or listen to tunes resonating through the tranquil building.

Live music events and performances on Naoshima add a colorful and enriching element to the island's cultural scene. Accept the beats of live music, lose yourself in the enthralling shows, and find the undiscovered beauties of Naoshima's artistic landscape.

11. Day Trips And Islands From Naoshima

11.1 Island of Teshima

Tucked away in the calm waters of the Seto Inland Sea, Teshima Island is a mesmerizing location that skillfully combines tranquility, art, and nature. Teshima, only a short boat journey from Naoshima, is the perfect place for a day trip or more extensive exploration because it offers a distinctive combination of modern artwork, beautiful scenery, and a laid-back environment.

A. **Introduction to Art among Scenic Beauty**

Teshima Island is well known for its tasteful blending of art and environment. Numerous long-term artworks by well-known artists may be found on the island, including:

1. * **Teshima Art Museum:** Architect Ryue Nishizawa created this simple concrete building with a permanent exhibit by artist Rei Naito that combines music and light to create a captivating interplay.

2. * **Les Archives du Coeur (Heart Archives):** Housed in a charming beachside structure, this artwork by Christian Boltanski offers a moving meditation on human connection by gathering and playing recordings of heartbeats from all over the world.

3. * **Matrix:** A site-specific creation by Shinro Ohtake, this artwork reflects the island's agricultural past by blending in perfectly with the surrounding rice terraces.

B. **Uncovering the Natural Wonders of Teshima**

Explore Teshima Island's abundant natural beauty beyond its art installations:

1. * **Hike and Bike Trails:** Travel the island's well-kept hiking and biking paths, which meander through verdant forests, picturesque hills, and quaint villages, to uncover its hidden treasures.

2. * **Rice Paddy Terraces:** Take in the peace of Teshima's rice paddy terraces while admiring the lush surroundings and the agricultural legacy of the island.

3. **Serene Beaches and Coastal Walks:** Take strolls along Teshima's shoreline while taking in the stunning vistas of the Seto Inland Sea and the cool sea wind. Find quiet coves and immaculate beaches that are ideal for leisurely moments.

C. **Teshima Island Day Trip Essentials**

1. * **Ferry Schedule:** Check the ferry schedules and available modes of transportation between Naoshima and Teshima to plan your day excursion.

2. * **Rental Bicycles:** Take into consideration renting a bicycle to tour the island independently and find undiscovered treasures off the usual route.

3. * **Picnic Essentials:** Take along some snacks or a picnic meal to savor the island's scenic surroundings.

4. * **Comfy Footwear:** When walking, hiking, or cycling on the island's many paths, wear comfy shoes.

5. * **Respectful Exploration:** Take care to leave no evidence of your presence, being sensitive to the island's natural ecosystem and local communities.

Teshima provides a special fusion of experiences that will rejuvenate, inspire, and reawaken your sense of the Seto Inland Sea's magnificence.

11.2 Island of Inujima

Situated in the Seto Inland Sea, Inujima Island is a charming island that provides a peaceful, artistic, and natural haven for visitors. Inujima, which is only a short boat journey from Naoshima, is the perfect place for a day vacation or longer stay since it harmoniously combines modern art installations, peaceful scenery, and a laid-back vibe to reveal its secrets.

A.   **Creative Expressions in Balance with Environment**

Thought-provoking artworks that blend in well with the island's natural beauty are displayed on Inujima Island. Discover the artistic treasures of the island, such as:

1. * **Setoda Art House:** Designed by architect Tadao Ando, this former elementary school is now an art space with a collection of installations by different artists exploring themes of memory, time, and human connection, such as Shinro Ohtake and Yukinori Yanagi.

2. * **Inujima Setoda Art Museum:** Featuring pieces by Hiroshi Sugimoto and Lucio Dal Fabbro, this museum was created by SANAA architects and has a

glass-walled, minimalistic structure that blurs the lines between art and nature.

3. * **Inujima Village House Project:** This ongoing project aims to create a distinctive fusion of art and architecture by renovating traditional Japanese houses into art spaces. Notable architects such as Tadao Ando and Junya Ishigami have contributed to the transformation of each house.

B. **Uncovering the Natural Beauty of Inujima**

In addition to its artistic appeal, Inujima Island has a serene natural setting that offers a much-needed break:

1. * **Calm Coastal Walks:** Take strolls along the shoreline of Inujima, soaking in the cool sea breeze and relishing the expansive views of the Seto Inland Sea.

2. * **Hidden Cove Adventures:** Explore the island's remote coves to find undiscovered rocky formations and

beaches that are ideal for quiet moments of contemplation.

3. Discover the network of Inujima's nature paths, which meander through verdant forests and rise to picturesque hilltops that provide breathtaking views of the nearby islands and the Seto Inland Sea.

C. **Organizing Your Inujima Island Day Trip**

1. * **Ferry Schedule:** Check the ferry schedules and available modes of transportation between Naoshima and Inujima to plan your day excursion.

2. * **Rental Bicycles:** To go around the island quickly and discover hidden gems at your speed, think about hiring a bicycle.

3. * **Picnic Essentials:** Take along some snacks or a picnic meal to enjoy among the island's scenic surroundings.

4. * **Comfortable Attire:** If you plan to walk, hike, or ride on the island's trails, wear comfortable clothing and shoes.

5. * **Island Etiquette:** Respect the locals and the peaceful environment of the island by leaving no evidence of your stay.

Inujima Island invites guests to experience a mesmerizing fusion of peace, nature, and art. From its peaceful vistas to its provocative art installations.

11.3 Island of Shodoshima

A mesmerizing jewel in the Seto Inland Sea, Shodoshima Island greets guests with a harmonic fusion of artistic expression, cultural history, and natural grandeur. Shodoshima, which is only a short ferry journey from Naoshima, provides a wide range of experiences, from exploring its untamed shoreline and lush hills to taking in its rich creative traditions and sampling its regional cuisine.

A. *A Tour through the Armor of Nature**

The natural splendor of Shodoshima Island is a visual feast for the senses. Explore its varied landscapes, which include:

1. * **Kankakei Gorge:** Take a leisurely trek through the picturesque Kankakei Gorge, where waterfalls tumble down stony cliffs amid verdant foliage, producing an amazing natural show.

2. Unwind on the immaculate sands of Oniishi Beach, which is well-known for its unusual "Devilish Rocks" formations that have been fashioned by the sea over millennia.

3. * **Shodoshima Olive Grove:** Discover the rich agricultural history of Shodoshima, an island known for producing olive oil, as you stroll through its aromatic olive orchards.

B. **Cultural Gems and Creative Pleasures**

For those who love the arts and culture, Shodoshima Island is a sanctuary. Discover its traditional treasures and creative gems, such as:

1. * **The Kinrin-an Art Museum:** Located in a restored traditional Japanese home, the Kinrin-an Art Museum offers a comprehensive introduction to contemporary art, including pieces by well-known artists such as Yayoi Kusama and Tadashi Kawamata.

2. * **Shodoshima Manga Museum:** Explore the world of manga at this museum, which features pieces by well-known manga artists and highlights the rich history of manga on the island.

3. * * Uchiwa Museum: Learn about the history and craftsmanship of traditional Japanese fans, or Uchiwa, and even make your own at this museum dedicated to the art form.

C. **Delicious Foods and Island Tastes**

The indigenous cuisine and culinary customs of Shodoshima Island entice the senses:

1.* **Shodoshima Olive Somen:** Savor the distinct flavor of this refreshing and traditional island treat—thin wheat noodles served in a chilled broth infused with olive oil.

2. * **Shodoshima Lemon Products:** Savor the zesty flavors of Shodoshima's lemons, which are used to make a range of goods, including ice cream, pastries, and alcoholic beverages.

3. * **Shodoshima Sea Bream:** Savor the subtle flavors of this locally renowned delicacy, which is renowned for its freshness and culinary adaptability.

D **Organizing Your Shodoshima Island Adventure**

1. * **Ferry Schedule:** To make the most of your visit planning, check the ferry schedules and available modes of transportation between Naoshima and Shodoshima.

2. * **Rental Bicycles and Buses:** To get around quickly and discover hidden gems, think about renting a bicycle or taking advantage of the island's bus system.

3. * **Location Options:** To suit a range of tastes and price points, select from a selection of lodging options, including contemporary hotels and traditional Japanese guesthouses.

4. * **Respectful Exploration:** Take care to protect the island's unspoiled ecosystem and traditional customs while also acknowledging its natural beauty.

11.4 City of Okayama

Okayama City, tucked away in Okayama Prefecture's scenic surroundings, entices tourists with a plethora of cultural attractions, a thriving food scene, and stunning natural surroundings. Okayama, which is conveniently located near Naoshima and offers a seamless combination of urban experience and peaceful getaways, is a great place to visit for a day trip or extended stay.

A. **Historical Jewels and Cultural Delights**

Okayama City is brimming with historical treasures and cultural attractions, such as:

1.* **Okayama Castle:** Take in the magnificence of Okayama Castle, also referred to as the "Crow Castle" because of its facade painted in black, a reminder of the city's feudal past.

2. * **Korakuen Garden**: Take a stroll around this beautiful Japanese landscape garden, a masterwork of landscape design, and take in its serene ponds, finely trimmed trees, and traditional teahouses.

3. * **Okayama Art Museum:** This museum offers a vast collection of Western and Japanese artwork, including pieces by Monet, Renoir, and El Greco. Come immerse yourself in the world of art.

B. **Tastes of the Region and Culinary Adventures**

Okayama City entices the palate with a thriving food scene and regional specialties, such as:

1. * **Bara Chirashi:** Savor the mouthwatering flavors of this iconic Okayama specialty, Bara Chirashi, a visually spectacular meal of heaping portions of fresh seafood and vegetables heaped over rice.

2. * **Kibidango:** A local favorite, kibidango is a traditional Japanese dessert fashioned from glutinous rice and filled with sweet bean paste. Savour its sweet and chewy sweetness.

3. * **Momiji Manju:** Savor the subtle flavors of Momiji Manju, which are well-known as souvenirs and are maple leaf-shaped cakes filled with sweet bean paste. Momiji Manju is an emblem of Okayama City.

C. **Serene Getaways and Natural Wonders**

Okayama City's intriguing natural attractions provide a welcome escape from the bustle of the city.

1. * **Kibitsu Shrine and Saikoji Temple:** Take a spiritual excursion to Kibitsu Shrine, renowned for its vivid fall foliage, and Saikoji Temple, one of the 88 temples of the Shikoku Pilgrimage.

2. **Okayama Museum of Natural Science:** Explore the wonders of nature at Okayama Museum of Natural Science, which features an extensive collection of animals, plants, and fossils, including the well-known "Giant Dinosaur".

3. * **Kamo Riverboat:** Take a leisurely boat down the Kamo River while taking in the serene riverbank surroundings and stunning views of the city skyline.

D. **Organizing Your Okayama City Adventure**

1.* **Transportation Options:** Okayama City's numerous areas and attractions are easily navigable and explorable thanks to the city's robust train and bus networks.

2. * **Location Options:** To suit a range of tastes and price points, pick from a selection of lodging options, including contemporary hotels and traditional Japanese ryokan inns.

3. * **Festivals and Events:** To fully immerse yourself in the city's colorful cultural traditions, check the local calendar for forthcoming festivals and events, including the Okayama Tanabata Festival and the Momijimatsuri (Autumn Leaf Festival).

4. * **Respectful Exploration:** To protect the city's natural beauty and cultural legacy, respect local customs and traditions, and leave no record of your stay.

Okayama City welcomes guests to experience its gastronomic delights, natural beauties, and rich cultural tapestry on a tour. Okayama provides a wide variety of experiences that will leave you feeling enriched, inspired, and strongly linked to the city's distinct charm. These experiences range from its historical buildings and artistic treasures to its delicious cuisine and tranquil scenery.

12. Naoshima Itinerary for Seven Days

12.1 Day 1: Welcome and Miyanoura Area Exploration

The first day on Naoshima is spent getting used to the island's artistic atmosphere and the quaint Miyanoura neighborhood. Take a stroll around Miyanoura Port to start your adventure, taking in the maritime ambiance and getting glimpses of Yayoi Kusama's famed Red Pumpkin, a whimsical art installation.

See the art-infused Naoshima Bath to experience a tranquil soak that sets the tone for the island's distinctive fusion of leisure and culture. In Miyanoura, sample the local fare at charming restaurants serving fresh seafood and traditional Japanese delicacies.

Explore the Art House Project in the Miyanoura neighborhood as the day goes on. These renovated traditional homes are home to fascinating modern art exhibits. Get involved in the neighborhood by going to a workshop or gallery talk to strengthen your bond with Naoshima's creative spirit.

Take a stroll along the shoreline at sunset to observe the Seto Inland Sea's shifting hues. An immersive week on Naoshima is set in motion by Miyanoura's fascinating fusion of art, culture, and coastal beauty.

12.2 Day 2: Visits to Benesse House Museum and Chichu Art Museum

The Benesse House Museum and the Chichu Art Museum are the two main attractions of Day 2. Begin at the architectural marvel of Tadao Ando, the Chichu Art Museum. Masterpieces by Claude Monet and James Turrell are housed in an underground museum that blends in perfectly with the surrounding environment. Chichu's mix of light and space makes for a captivating experience.

Head to the Benesse House Museum, a tasteful fusion of modern art and luxury lodging, following a fine lunch at the museum's café. Discover its varied galleries, which include pieces by artists like David Hockney and Andy Warhol. Surrounded by beautiful greenery, the museum's architecture perfectly accentuates the carefully chosen artwork inside.

Enjoy a last glimpse of the day as the sun sets over the Benesse House Oval while thinking back on the meaningful creative exchanges that shape Naoshima's rich cultural legacy.

12.3 Day 3: Honmura Area and Art House Project

On Day 3, take a deep dive into the Art House Project by exploring the Honmura neighborhood. Explore remodeled historic homes that serve as canvases for various artistic endeavors. Highlights are the Minamidera, a unique sensory experience designed by

James Turrell, and the Kadoya House, with its ethereal light works.

In Honmura, enjoy a traditional Japanese lunch while taking in the flavors of the area amid the picturesque streets. Explore the Honmura Lounge & Archive for more information about the origins and development of the Art House Project.

Finish the day with a stroll through Honmura's small streets, where you may interact with the island's small community and find hidden pieces of art. As the day comes to an end, consider how well modern art has blended into Naoshima's rich history.

12.4 Day 4: Full-Day Trip to Teshima Island

Day 4: Take a fascinating day trip to Teshima Island, which is only a short ferry journey from Naoshima. Visit the Teshima Art Museum, an architectural wonder encircled by olive trees and providing a view of the Seto

Inland Sea, to start your exploration. An immersive experience is produced by the museum's open layout and dynamic relationship with the natural environment.

Discover the many art installations by Teshima on the island, such as the Teshima Yokoo House, an Art House Project location that features Tadanori Yokoo's creations. The small size of the island makes it possible to take strolls or leisurely bicycle rides between locations, offering chances to find hidden treasures.

Have a delicious midday meal at one of the neighborhood restaurants in Teshima, maybe savoring some olive-infused cuisine. The island's dedication to sustainability, demonstrated by its terraced rice fields and environmentally beneficial projects, enhances the value of your trip.

As the day draws to a close, savor the peaceful atmosphere of Teshima and consider how art has been skillfully incorporated into the island's unspoiled beauty. Your overall tour of the cultural archipelago of the Seto

Inland Sea is enhanced by the Teshima experience, with its artistic marvels and tranquil settings.

12.5 Day 5: Beach Time and Outdoor Activities

Day 5 allows you to experience Naoshima's outdoor allure. Take a beautiful trek in the morning, maybe climbing the hills to get sweeping views of the Seto Inland Sea. The island's well-landscaped walking pathways provide the ideal mix of outdoor recreation and natural surroundings.

Visit one of Naoshima's immaculate beaches for a leisurely afternoon by the water after an energetic morning. Admire the beauty of the seaside, curl up with a nice book, or just soak up the sun. Naoshima's beaches are a tranquil haven that offers an alternative viewpoint to the days' art-focused activities.

Enjoy fresh seafood and regional delicacies while exploring the neighborhood's coastal eateries for lunch.

Consider hiring a bicycle in the afternoon to travel to the island's more isolated areas, where you can find hidden art installations and enjoy the leisurely pace of island life.

Enjoy dinner by the sea while you think back on the easy transition from immersing yourself in art to relaxing outside as the day comes to an end. Day 5 showcases Naoshima's versatility and its appeal to both culture vultures and those looking for peace in the natural world.

Day 6 of 12.6: Ando Museum and Lee Ufan Museum

Explore Naoshima's creative treasures on Day 6 by going to the Lee Ufan Museum. Tadao Ando's architectural masterpiece, which houses Korean artist Lee Ufan's artwork. The calm environment and simple architecture of the museum create an engrossing area for reflection and art-related interaction.

Explore the Ando Museum, which is devoted to the famous architect Tadao Ando himself, after spending the morning at the Lee Ufan Museum. Learn about the architectural philosophy that shaped Naoshima's cultural landscape and Ando's creative process.

Consider having lunch at one of the museums' restaurants to savor delicious food surrounded by carefully chosen artwork and architectural design. In the afternoon, you can take in the island's constantly changing artistic tapestry by visiting your favorite installations or discovering new ones.

As the sun goes down, pause to consider the meaningful experiences you had with the local art and architecture while visiting Naoshima. The devotion of the island to promoting a conversation between nature, art, and the human spirit is best summed up on Day 6.

12.7 Day 7: Farewell and Last Investigations

Make the most of your departure by fitting in some last-minute explorations on your last day. Start the day with a leisurely walk around Miyanoura, returning to some of your favorite locations or exploring some new ones. Talk to the local craftsmen and consider buying a one-of-a-kind souvenir to remember your time in Naoshima.

Savor the subtleties of Naoshima's artistic history by spending some time exploring any hidden art installations or Art House Project venues before you leave. If you have time, take a goodbye dinner at one of the island's quaint restaurants and savor the delicacies that characterize this oasis of culture.

Take with you the memories of Naoshima's artistic marvels, scenic splendor, and tasteful blend of innovation and tradition as you wish it goodnight. Take off feeling appreciative of the life-changing experience

that took place on this lovely island in the Seto Inland
Sea.

13. Useful Advice And Information For Naoshima

13.1 Information and Visitor Centers:

The well-planned Visitor Centers and Information hubs in Naoshima, a treasure in the Seto Inland Sea, are essential to enabling this exploration. Naoshima offers a significant artistic and cultural experience. These hubs go beyond their conventional functions, becoming cultural gatekeepers that act as catalysts for a greater comprehension of the island's creative assets in addition to offering maps and brochures.

These facilities, which are well-positioned across Naoshima, have friendly staff members who are enthusiastic about introducing visitors to the island's rich cultural legacy. Based on their interests, visitors may anticipate tailored recommendations that will turn their trip into a carefully planned experience. Naoshima uses state-of-the-art technology in these centers to disseminate information beyond traditional means, providing immersive stories about the numerous art pieces strewn over the island through interactive displays and digital guides.

A deeper level of understanding is provided by the Visitor Center-organized guided tours, which reveal the historical and cultural background of the artworks. These tours' immersive format creates a strong bond between guests and the creative manifestations that characterize Naoshima. Essentially, the Visitor Centers transcend beyond being informational centers and take on the role of cultural curators, molding the story of a visitor's journey and creating a permanent bond with Naoshima's spirit.

13.2 Safety Advice and Contact Information:

Naoshima places a high priority on safety, and the island's dedication to providing a secure environment for its guests is demonstrated by the extensive list of safety advice and emergency services available. Everyone who visits this creative sanctuary, from art lovers to casual visitors, gains from these initiatives that improve the general well-being of people who do so.

1. Guidelines for Artistic Exploration: Naoshima promotes polite engagement and responsible exploration of its art installations. The safety of visitors and the preservation of these priceless cultural artifacts are guaranteed when they follow the prescribed walkways and avoid touching the artwork.

2. Weather Preparation: Visitors are urged to come prepared for the wide range of weather that can occur in Naoshima. Having necessities like water, sunscreen, and rain gear with you helps ensure a safe and enjoyable exploration of the island's natural beauties.

3. Emergency Services: Naoshima has well-positioned police stations and hospitals, so in the event of an emergency, help will be provided quickly. Staff who speak more than one language help to demonstrate the

island's dedication to visitor safety by enabling efficient communication with non-Japanese speakers in an emergency.

4. Collaborative Safety Culture: Naoshima encourages visitors to report safety concerns as soon as they arise, fostering a sense of communal responsibility. This cooperative strategy contributes to a setting where everyone can safely appreciate the creative offerings by reinforcing the notion that safety is a shared responsibility.

5. Signage and Directions: Visitors are guided on emergency procedures and safety precautions by prominent signage located throughout Naoshima. Adhering to these guidelines improves security and makes for a safe and enjoyable exploration experience.

13.3 Pharmacies and Medical Facilities:

Naoshima's vast network of pharmacies and medical services reflects its commitment to the welfare of its visitors. Visitors can confidently immerse themselves in the island's artistic and natural treasures, knowing that their health requirements will be well-catered for.

1. Medical Infrastructure: Naoshima is home to modern clinics and hospitals with staff members who are qualified to handle a variety of medical issues. Because of the island's dedication to providing top-notch healthcare, guests may be sure to obtain trustworthy medical treatment while visiting.

2. Pharmacies and Medical Supplies: A range of over-the-counter drugs and medical supplies are available at the pharmacies in Naoshima. These facilities serve a variety of medical needs, from minor illnesses to necessary treatments, so guests may take care of health issues quickly and easily.

3. Multilingual Staff: Naoshima frequently offers multilingual staff in medical facilities and pharmacies, acknowledging the worldwide nature of its tourists. This well-considered innovation guarantees clear

communication, allaying worries for non-Japanese speakers requesting medical attention.

4. Visitor Assurance: Naoshima's attitude to pharmacies and medical services goes beyond utilitarianism; it symbolizes the island's dedication to hospitality. It is possible for visitors to fully immerse themselves in the artistic marvels of Naoshima, knowing that their health requirements are taken seriously and well-cared for, thanks to the combination of dependable healthcare services and a courteous, knowledgeable approach to tourist well-being.

13.4 Etiquette and Customs:

Immersed in cultural diversity, Naoshima upholds a set of traditions and manners that enhance the experience of visitors. To fully immerse oneself in the allure of this island decorated with modern art and breathtaking scenery, visitors must comprehend and respect the local customs.

1. Courtesies and Respect: Courtesies and respect are highly valued in Japanese society. It is traditional for visitors to extend a bow of courtesy to natives upon meeting them. This small gesture acknowledges the island's cultural past and promotes a pleasant attitude.

2. Shoes Off Indoors: The Japanese habit of taking off shoes before entering indoor areas is followed by many establishments, including art venues and traditional inns. Visitors should be ready to adhere to this custom, which is frequently made easier by the slippers that are supplied.

3. Photography etiquette: Although there are many beautiful sights in Naoshima, some art pieces may prohibit photos. To respect the artist's aim and maintain the integrity of the artwork, it is imperative to pay attention to signage and standards.

4. Calm Appreciation: The calm atmosphere of Naoshima encourages introspection. It is recommended that visitors take a thoughtful approach to appreciating

the art and the natural surroundings, avoiding noisy conversations and disruptive activity.

4. Trash Disposal: Tight waste separation regulations exist in Japan. To support the island's efforts to maintain a sustainable environment, guests should be careful to separate their rubbish into appropriate categories.

By adhering to these traditions and manners, tourists not only respect the native way of life but also promote harmony between the island's inhabitants, the arts, and the natural world.

13.5 Connectivity and Internet Options:

Even with its quiet, isolated attractiveness, Naoshima understands the value of connectivity in the contemporary world. To enable tourists to remain connected while taking in the island's artistic and natural attractions, a range of internet and connectivity alternatives are available.

1. Wi-Fi Hotspots: Free Wi-Fi hotspots are available in a lot of public areas, such as cafés and museums. Visitors can obtain maps, exchange experiences, and maintain contact with the outside world at these centers.

2. Local SIM Cards: You can get local SIM cards if you're looking for continuous access. With the data plans these cards provide, guests can use their smartphones for communication and navigation the entire time they are there.

3. Internet cafés: High-speed internet and PCs are available to guests at the internet cafés in Naoshima. These areas serve people who might not have carried their electronics with them or who require a specific place to work.

4. Connectivity at Lodgings: Guesthouses and hotels in Naoshima usually provide free Wi-Fi to their patrons. This guarantees that, following a day of adventure, guests may relax and tell their friends and family about their experiences.

Although Naoshima promotes disengaging from the hectic pace of everyday life, these internet choices offer a counterbalance by enabling tourists to record and share their experiences without detracting from the serene ambiance of the island.

13.6 Taking Accessibility Into Account:

Situated in the middle of the Seto Inland Sea, Naoshima is dedicated to providing everyone with access to its creative treasures. The island accommodates a range of accessibility requirements so that guests with different abilities and backgrounds can enjoy its cultural attractions.

1. Wheelchair accessibility is a priority in the design of many public areas and art spaces in Naoshima. Accessible transportation options such as ramps and elevators make it possible for all visitors to discover the artistic marvels of the island.

2. Information in Several Languages: Naoshima offers information in several languages in recognition of its global readership. This improves the island's overall accessibility and provides support to non-Japanese speakers through signage, pamphlets, and digital guides.

3. Assistance for Special Needs: Guests with particular requirements or impairments can make a prior request for assistance. The island is dedicated to creating a friendly atmosphere, and employees are frequently prepared to assist guests with particular needs to guarantee a smooth visit.

4. Transportation Options: Naoshima offers buses and ferries that are specially equipped to accommodate people with limited mobility. To help visitors plan their trips, clear information regarding accessible routes and services is easily accessible.

Naoshima's commitment to accessibility goes beyond compliance; it is an authentic expression of inclusivity, guaranteeing that all individuals, irrespective of their background or physical capabilities, can participate in the artistic and cultural fabric of the island.

Made in the USA
Las Vegas, NV
31 October 2024

10828313R30098